Inspiring Designs for
NEEDLEPOINT

CLARE MUZZATTI

KANGAROO PRESS

INSPIRING DESIGNS FOR NEEDLEPOINT
First published in Australia in 2005 by Kangaroo Press
An imprint of Simon & Schuster (Australia) Pty Limited
Suite 2, Lower Ground Floor,
14-16 Suakin Street,
Pymble NSW 2073

A Viacom Company
Sydney New York London Toronto

Visit our website at www.simonsaysaustralia.com

Cataloguing-in-Publication data:

Muzzatti, Clare.
        Inspiring designs for needlepoint.

        Includes index.
        ISBN 0 7318 1246 8.

        1. Canvas embroidery - Patterns. 2. Needlework - Patterns.
        I. Title.

        746.442

Cover and internal design by Anna Warren, Warren Ventures Pty Ltd
Typeset in Sabon 10/15pt
Printed in China through Colorcraft Ltd, Hong Kong

10 9 8 7 6 5 4 3 2 1

Contents

*B = Beginner, I = Intermediate, A = Advanced

Introduction

Welcome to needlepoint! What this book will show you is how, with a range of wool, silks and cottons, a lively and artistic world can be yours. This book offers a guiding hand to those who wish to discover what they can create and the projects are aimed to seduce the reader into 'giving it a go'. Some readers will have already mastered Tent stitch or intricate cross stitch patterns, while others may have just discovered this new and interesting art form. It really does not matter whether you know anything about needlepoint or not, because 'doing' is a great teacher. Much of my knowledge comes from solving problems as they arose, and from reading books on related topics.

Just as an engrossing novel can consume you, 'reading' an artwork can rescue you from your inner voice of daily concerns. Creating an artwork with stitching massages the mind, untangles tension, soothes fear and leaves you at peace.

This is a book about love. I am passionate about needlepoint. I have fallen deeply in love with colour, texture and the world of creation. I enjoy melding ideas and subjects to produce interesting juxtapositions. But above all I wish to pass on to you what I have experienced and learnt.

My needlepoint method

The work in this book is what I call 'needlepoint' rather than tapestry. In my mind tapestry is associated with the printed canvases of DMC, Semco, Baxter etc. It is sold as a standard product, printed by the thousand and commercially available on both sides of the world.

The following projects are designs I have developed for you to reproduce or use as jumping-off points for producing your own needlepoint creation. The method is quite simple. First work out a design on paper, then with a waterproof pen trace the design onto the canvas. Next paint in the colours with acrylic paint and finally stitch over the painting in a wide range of coloured threads to create subtle shades and dramatic contrasts. This is a very free method and doesn't straitjacket you into counting the stitches on a chart. Only the Bacchus project in this book is worked from a counted chart and that is because it is a face and needs to be accurate. Otherwise, feel free to take liberties with all the designs. Information and all the tips you will need for creating your own canvases are presented in Chapters 2 and 3.

Each project has stitch instructions, an outline drawing of the design for tracing or copying onto a canvas, and a colour chart showing exactly which shades of thread to use. There is also a colour photograph of each finished piece.

The projects are big enough to create an impact but can still be completed fairly quickly. They are easily portable, lightweight, and cool to work in warm weather.

A little history

The term 'tapestry' originally meant a woven wall hanging or covering. It was created on tall wooden looms by weavers and was a furnishing only afforded by the rich. Even today tapestries are still being made by hand, and as in the past, they are large, labour intensive and very expensive, making them only affordable for the wealthy or government. However, despite the enormous amount of time and expense involved, a hand woven tapestry can be stunning.

In Australia, the term 'tapestry' has come to mean 'canvas' or 'Berlin' work. This change in meaning occurred when The Cambridge Tapestry Company (founded in 1898) produced a large range of painted canvases based on antique designs. The period flavour of these designs was very popular, and so the term 'tapestry' was linked to canvas work. Previously, such work on canvas had been called 'Berlin wool work'. The design was stitched on plain canvas using a printed chart. The leading publisher in this area was a Berliner named Wittich, who produced designs of flowers, birds, animals and other exotic images. Canvas work before the age of Wittich existed in a world where learning was by rote and example.

In the past, exact replication of a 'Masters' artwork was highly valued. At Como House in Melbourne hangs a copy of Louis David's painting 'Napoleon Crossing the Alps'. It was first painted on very fine canvas and then worked in petit point with silk and wool. It dates from 1802–1807.

Such painstaking work and devotion was respected and admired. In a time before photographs, when travel to Australia from Europe involved a perilous voyage of several months, it had a currency that has been forgotten over time. As a political statement, the impact of an image of Napoleon at the height of his political power had more than a smack of republicanism. However, in today's eyes, as Marion Fletcher points out in her book *Needlework in Australia* (published in Melbourne by Oxford University Press, 1989): 'There is a lot of doubt as to the value of this meticulous but uncreative work as an exercise in needlework'.

This is a strong comment and in part reflects a change in our values. Today we rarely consider the context in which an artifact is produced. We tend not to value the determination of an individual to complete a work nor the countless hours devoted to improving their craft skills. Where a machine will do it with speed and economy, we are seduced by convenience and thrift.

Sad to say, Marion Fletcher's view of tapestry has validity. Second-hand shops, charity stores and rummage sales usually sport an unloved and discarded tapestry or two. It appears as though fashion has firmly closed the door on this type of needlework. The main reason being that it appears mindless to stitch a pattern already provided as a printed design. Also, many of the printed designs in commercial production have been produced for years, with designs which range from gaudy and childlike to darker classical subjects—the Australian market has been awash with these for too long.

So what is the future for needlepoint? Fortunately, there is a growing trend overseas towards original designs, hand painted on canvases. They are sold on the internet and are priced as works of art, ranging from a few hundred to over a thousand US dollars. But rather than pay hundreds of dollars for an original work, why not create your own distinct designs? Armed with the information from this book, you now can. So take up the challenge and create your own one-off needlepoint original.

CHAPTER 1
Getting Started

Materials: *canvas; threads; a ribbon long enough to bind the edge of the canvas.*

Tools: *needles; sharp scissors; stitch ripper; snaplock bags for storage; ruler; waterproof pen; sewing machine (optional)*

Before beginning, make sure you have clean hands, good sunlight or lamplight, and a clean area in which to work.

Materials
Canvas
There are many types of canvas, but the three best known are as follows:

Penelope
This canvas is commonly used in commercially printed canvases. Its weave features pairs of threads woven at right angles to each other and stiffened with glue or sizing to keep them in place. The pairs of threads can be pushed apart, enabling finer work in areas where greater detail is required, such as facial features. It is suitable for diagonal stitches but, unless you do not mind the canvas showing through, it is not suitable for Long stitch. However, the well-known artist Kaffe Fasset (see his book *Glorious Inspiration*, published by Random House, UK, 1991) uses Long stitch and reveals the canvas to great effect.

Mono
This canvas uses single threads laid at right angles and held in place with size.

Cheap versions of Penelope and mono are available in both plain and printed forms, but avoid these as they unravel easily and are not very durable.

Interlock
Once discovered and used, interlock canvas will be a favourite. It looks like mono canvas but on closer inspection reveals pairs of threads twisted around each other whilst crossing over at right angles. As a result, the canvas is more stable when damp or softened through handling, and the cut edge is less likely to unravel. It is stronger than mono and can be used for furnishing projects. Interlock can be used for diagonal and Straight stitches. All the work in this book has been stitched on Zweigart Interlock.

Plain canvas is usually sold cut from a roll. Before buying look out for weak or broken threads, as well as knots. All threads should lie straight and at right angles to each other. Check that both sides of the canvas are clean and unmarked. Ensure that the person cutting the canvas cuts in line with the threads (this is necessary if the previous cut was crooked). Finally, roll the canvas up if it is a large piece and protect it with plastic or paper. Once home, iron it with a warm iron to prevent it from curling.

Count
Canvases are manufactured in a range of sizes known as the 'count': the number of holes per square inch. The smaller the hole, the higher the number of the count and the finer the canvas. The most commonly used counts are 22, 18, 14, 10 and 7. The designs in this book use 18 count, which allows for detail and subtle colour changes. It is the equivalent of cross stitch in scale, but with half the stitches. 14 count is the next largest and is still useful for more detailed areas and shading. 10 count is very easy on the eye, it produces bold images where detail is often lost in shadow or simplified to the point of becoming cartoon-like.

10 count is excellent for domestic items such as cushions. A strong, colour-fast, mothproof woollen thread is value for money in tackling such work. The largest counts, 8 and 7, are reserved for rug-making, and use knitting and carpet wool.

Whether you are taking up needlepoint as an art form or simply for pleasure, the most basic and important concept to consider is your own physical limitations. The canvas hole size and threads must suit your level of vision. A fine mesh canvas has several excellent qualities: the projects are smaller, lightweight and—when heat and humidity are a consideration—a lot cooler to work with. The threads are smooth and fine (especially if you use silk). The drawback, however, is that its size can strain the eyes, in which case try 14 count, and if this is still uncomfortable try 10 count.

Daylight is best to work in, with a quality halogen lamp a close second. Fluorescent light is adequate, but not perfect as it changes the tone of the colours you are working with, so never choose a colour under fluorescent light.

Some 10 count canvases have a tendency to stiffness and a rough feel. Rolling the canvas up in each direction and gently squeezing it will generally soften it. If it is still too rough, give it a brief and gentle dip in a bath of cold water, then roll it up in a soft towel to remove excess water. Unroll and leave it to dry in the shade. It will shrink, as all cotton fabrics do, but being an interlock canvas it will neither distort nor fray. When the work is blocked and stretched replace the size you washed out with a fabric stiffener.

Thread

In this book thread is described as strands, threads and skeins.* If you think of the smallest unit being a filament, then:

- a *strand* is made up of two or more filaments
- a *thread* is made up of two or more strands
- a *skein* is usually 5–8 metres long

- a *hank* is much longer, perhaps 20 metres or more.

Silk thread is used straight from the skein. There are normally four strands in a silk thread. Cotton thread is made up of six strands; however, only four strands are used to make a thread for working on 18 count canvas. This means you will have to 'strip' the thread, and save the two unused strands for future use.

To strip a thread

Hold the thread in one hand and with the other gently pull out the strands one at a time from the twist of thread. If you wish, lay them out on a flat clean teatowel and iron them with a warm iron. These strands can now be mixed with other colours or used as 'single threads'.

Length of thread

Avoid the temptation to work with threads any longer than from your elbow to your wrist. The longer the strand, the more distance your arm must travel to complete the stitch. This will be tiring and it will also 'age' the thread by overworking it, leaving it looking uneven.

Remember: the more delicate the thread, the shorter the length and the simpler the stitch to be used.

Types of thread

The count of the canvas will to some extent dictate the thickness of the thread to be used. If the thickness is unsuitable it will either allow the canvas to show through or it will be difficult to slide the needle through the hole without tugging at the thread. All the designs featured in this book have thread lists. For threads that are unavailable others may be substituted, but before starting with a new brand always try it on a scrap of canvas to see if it gives good coverage. If it does, consider what other qualities it has: is it waterfast and colourfast? Can

*NOTE: In this book thread(s) is abbreviated to thd(s) and strand(s) is abbreviated to std(s).

it be split and mixed with other threads? Is it a standard colour or does it vary between dye lots? How robust is the thread—for example, is it suitable only for framed work? How easy is it to sew with? Some man-made threads are a challenge to use and require either some beeswax to stabilise the cut ends, or a quick wipe with a damp sponge to release the kinks.

If you buy threads with tags that must be removed before use, store both tag and thread in a bag labelled with the dye lot number. However, if the thread is delicate, such as silk, record the tag details on the bag.

With threads that are delicate, such as mohair, or temperamental such as some gold threads, there will be wastage. It is wiser to use short lengths of thread, 16 cm or less, discarding the needle end if it fluffs or thins, to avoid producing ragged work. This is why sewing on a scrap of canvas with untried thread will tell you so much.

The way strands are twisted together is another important feature. Many threads have a noticeable 'thread direction', which means that the thread will move more smoothly in one direction than in the other. Finding the thread direction means easier sewing. To find the direction, run the thread lightly between your fingers and thumb, first in one direction then in the opposite. One direction will feel smoother. This is the stitch direction and the end to thread your needle with. However, when using Madeira's Mouline, Silk, Decora and Metallic threads, please note that the packaging which keeps the thread clean and tangle free also presents it ready for threading on to the needle. The thread direction need not be applied to DMC Medicis Wool, which stitches as easily with a single thread doubled over in the needle as it does with two strands in the needle. It is my habit to slip the tags off the ends of the skein, untwist the wool and cut the circular hank. Then I rethread the dye lot tag onto the hank before folding it in half and twisting it into a loose knot. This keeps it in a tidy bundle and stops it from becoming entangled with other hanks.

Tools
Needles
Needlepoint uses a short blunt needle with an elongated eye, commonly called a 'tapestry needle'. The needle should slide easily through the hole of the canvas; it should never need to be pushed through. The higher the needle size, the finer the needle.

- Sizes 24 and 22 are suitable for 18 count canvas
- 20 and 18 are suitable for 10 count canvas

Gold-plated needles are favoured by some as they are said to slip through the canvas more easily. The best needle is a new one. Never use a needle that is corroded or has a rough feel, and never leave one

---

THREAD TIPS
- When using strands from two colours to produce a new tone, align the hanks, fold them in half and knot loosely, forming one bundle.
- Work dark colours first and white last.
- Accidents do happen. If your thread becomes wet, allow it to dry at its own pace on a clean towel in the shade. Soiled thread can be handwashed in a mild wool detergent in cold water with no agitation, but beware: some colours may run.
- Thread cut with sharp scissors is easier to pass through a fine needle.
- Never pull or tug the thread at the end of a stitch.
- If your thread tangles or knots behind your work, lift up the work and allow the threaded needle to dangle and untwist itself.

in a piece of work you have put aside. Needles left in the open air age and are not suitable for use. They also wear out, especially around the eye. If your thread continually catches in this area, a small fracture is likely to be the cause.

Scissors

It is well worth spending money on a good pair of scissors that will cut easily and cleanly. The blades should move smoothly past each other, yet give a slight sense of brushing each other when they meet. The blades must be straight and clean. Except in an emergency, never use them to cut anything apart from thread. Use kitchen scissors or an old pair of dressmaking shears to cut canvas.

Stitch ripper

The quickest way to unpick is to use a stitch ripper. The head is shaped like a claw: the long pointy end of the claw slides under the stitch between the thread and the canvas, lifting the thread away from the canvas before it is cut. Correctly used, the stitch ripper is safer and less likely to cut the canvas than scissors.

Snaplock bags

People who are passionate about their work are rarely far from it. Take your work on your travels in a simple plastic bag with a snaplock seal—it is waterproof, transparent and easily cleaned.

Ruler

A metric ruler is essential. Most designs in this book start with a ruled border, which follows the threads of the canvas, giving you a perfect frame in which to place the rest of the design.

Waterproof pen

Your pen must be waterproof so it will not bleed through to the thread if it gets wet. On 18 count canvas a 0.5 or a 0.8 black felt-tipped pen should be adequate.

Sewing machine

The edge of all canvas can be rough and may unravel. You can either tape the raw edge, though this can come adrift and leave a sticky residue, or machine sew a double-sided 4 cm wide satin ribbon folded in half lengthways over the edge of the canvas. There is no need to alter the top or bottom tension, just use the same tension you would for cotton fabric. Do this once you have painted the canvas.

CHAPTER 2

The stitches and techniques

The following directions are written for people who are right-handed. If you are left-handed, you may find it easier to reverse the start of the stitch and the stitch direction.

Tent stitch, also called Continental Tent stitch

This is one of three methods of creating a Tent stitch. It has been chosen for its raised padded effect, as well as for its ease and versatility in working around uneven shapes. Tent stitch is worked on the diagonal, with the stitching thread always crossing the intersection of the weft and warp threads of the canvas.

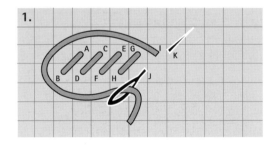

1. Bring the needle out at square A and return it at square B. Bring it to the front at square C beside square A and continue as shown. At the end of the row, bring the needle out of the hole beside your last stitch, turn your canvas 180° and continue stitching. Repeat going back and forth across the canvas area.

Stitch slowly until you develop some confidence, and always avoid pulling or tugging on the thread at the end of each stitch. It is better to allow the thread to relax in each stitch than to have it tensed and pulled taut, which will result in a warped canvas.

For the purists a slope to the right is better than a slope to the left. However, try both and choose whichever is most comfortable.

Stitch direction

Make sure that the stitch is done in the same direction for every row, with the front and the back of the canvas showing lines of sloping stitches. Work across the canvas in one direction only, and avoid making the rows horizontal in one area and vertical in another; otherwise the completed canvas will look uneven.

Starting and finishing a row of stitches

There is more than one method of starting a row of stitching, but this is the method I use. Bring the threaded needle up through the canvas leaving a 3 cm tail at the back. Begin to stitch, making sure that you capture the tail on the back by stitching over it until it is completely covered. Repeat this for every colour change. However, when using the same coloured thread, simply slip the needle through the back of four to five stitches in the row above. Hold the tail of the thread with your thumb as you start to stitch, and trim any excess with care. To finish, take the needle to the back of the work and slide it through the backs of the last five stitches. Trim the thread close to the stitching.

The back of your work

Needlepoint should be a pleasure, not a penance, so never become too disheartened with your work if it is untidy on the back. Among my treasures is the first canvas I ever did. From the front it shows the foal that I sketched, and apart from the fact that I stitched nearly to the edge of the canvas, it looks reasonably decent. The reverse is altogether different. It is a jumble of leaping threads, twisting and curling like a bizarre abstract painting. It is quite beautiful in its own way and certainly contains more wool than the front!

These days I am neater; I stitch the dominant colour first, and then slip in the odd stitches of contrasting tones. This is especially important when stitching a face—the areas of lighter tone should be stitched before the finer, darker detail. When working on two areas of the same colour separated by two or three stitches, a 'jump' can be made. This is best done by slipping the needle through the backs of the stitches in your path. Bigger jumps can be made using the same method, but the risk is that the thread linking the two areas will be so tight that the canvas cannot be stretched and blocked without undoing these sections and stitching them again.

Wheat stitch

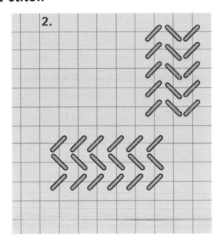

2. Wheat stitch is simply rows of Tent stitch that slope in opposite directions. These rows can be worked either horizontally or vertically.

Straight stitch

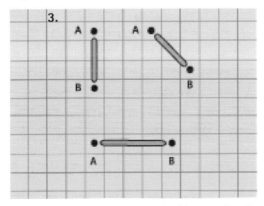

3. A simple stitch that can be worked in any direction and in various lengths. It is easily snagged and pulled, so leave it till last.

Long stitch

Long stitch is a repeated Straight stitch. In its simplest form it is either horizontal or vertical. Long stitch quickly covers the canvas with a padded effect. Take care, however, not to pull firmly at the end of the stitch, as this will distort the canvas.

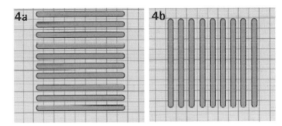

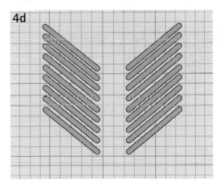

4a,b,c. Long stitch worked in opposite directions.

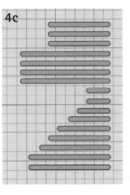

4d. Long stitch at the same angle as Tent stitch.

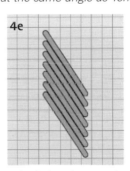

4e. Long stitch worked at a steep angle. Note that the threads lie closer. This angle is very useful when working with a narrow or delicate thread.

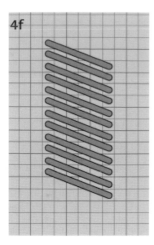

4f. Long stitch worked at a more shallow angle.

Padded Long stitch

This stitch technique is used only in the Rainforest project.

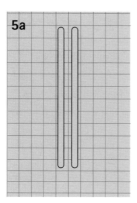

5a. Make vertical Long stitches.

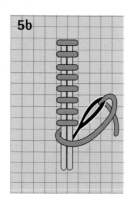 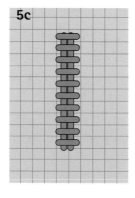

5b,c. Overstitch vertical stitches with short horizontal stitches. Note that the horizontal stitches exit and enter from the holes beneath the vertical threads.

French knots

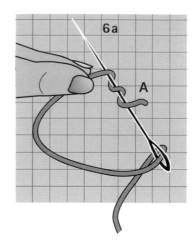

6a. Make a solid knot at the end of the thread and bring the needle through the canvas to the front at A. Hold the thread taut with the left hand and wind it once or twice clockwise around the tip of the needle.

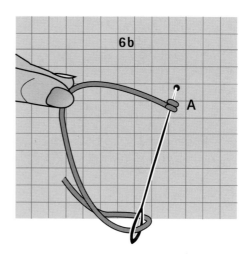

6b. Maintain the tension on the thread and gently push the needle back through the canvas at A while holding down the knot with your thumb. As you slide the needle back through the canvas, gently pull the thread through the knot, leaving the knot to sit on top of the canvas.

Bullion knots

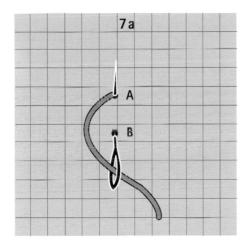

7a. Bring the needle out at A then re-enter the canvas at B, leaving a large loop. Next slide the point of the needle out at A.

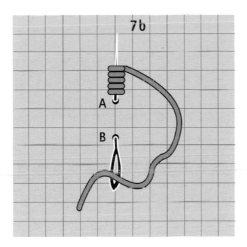

7b. Now place the tip of your left index finger under the needle to lift it away from the surface of the canvas and wrap the thread from the loop clockwise around the needle evenly five times with the right hand. Place the left thumb over the coil to keep it in place and gently slide the needle completely through to make the Bullion.

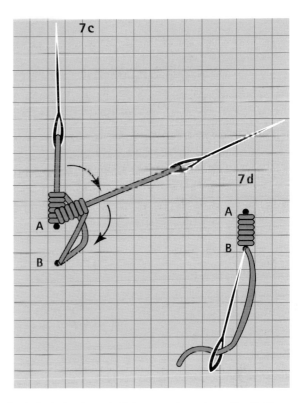

7c,d. Pull the thread all the way through so the Bullion lies evenly between A and B. To anchor the knot, pull the rest of the thread through and enter at B to secure at the back.

Thread blending

The designs in this book often link tones across large areas to produce subtle changes in colour. This technique relies on mixing two or more strands of different threads to make a new colour or to combine colours for a tweed-like area that melds, for example, forest with sky. To do this you first have to 'strip' the thread by holding one end of it and gently pulling one strand out of the top. Repeat this until all the strands are free. Thread stripping is usually used on cotton thread known as 'stranded cotton', some silks, such as Madeira Silk, and many metallic threads. Once stripped, the strands can be ironed. A single strand may be used on its own or added to other strands to produce a 'blend'. You can mix threads of different types, and in this book you will find metallic is blended with wool, and wool with silk. In this way new textures are also created, such as the feel and look of shantung silk in the background of the Toute Petite project.

Thread blending to create a gradual tonal transition is frequently used in this book. For example, suppose you are working with a silk thread made up of four strands: rows 1 and 2 could be in the original colour; rows 3 and 4 could be three strands of the original colour and one of a new colour; rows 5 and 6 could be two strands of each colour; and rows 7 and 8 could be one strand of the original and three strands of the new colour. Of course you can vary the effects by using more coloured strands; or by spreading tonal change over more rows to make it more gradual; or by using different types and textures of yarn.

Painting the canvas

Tools: *clean white towel, a set of brushes, a plastic palette, water, acrylic paints, textile medium.*

If the canvas is not perfectly flat, now is the time to iron it. Canvas can cope with some dampness but beware of wetting it, as once soaked it can shrink and lose the sizing that gives it rigidity. Always place a clean white towel or nappy under the canvas. It will absorb moisture and when you have finished painting it will peel away from the canvas without leaving a residue. Do not use paper towels, they will stick. A white towel will let you see your design clearly, though the paint on it will not come off in the wash!

Only a few paintbrushes are needed. These should be of good quality so that you can paint accurately along the outline. My favourites are Liqitex shaders no. 14 and no. 20. They have chisel-shaped heads of 1 cm and 2 cm respectively. Whatever brush you use, make sure it is not stiff and doesn't divide into groups of hairs when dry. Wash the brush the minute you finish using it, and at the end of a painting session massage a drop of detergent into the brush hairs to keep them soft. The properties that make the fabric medium stick the paint to the canvas can also gum up the brushes. The life of a brush will be extended if it is not dunked in paint up to the metal crimp that holds the hairs in place.

Paints

Acrylic craft paints are preferable to thinned oil paints as they are non-toxic and water soluble, and can be watered down and mixed with a textile medium. There are various brands available but I use Jo Sonja's. Only a small amount of paint is required: mix this with twice as much water and a drop of textile medium. Add less water for light colours and more water for dark colours to achieve an even wash. If you prefer a range of tones rather than an even wash, carefully dip the brush to different depths of your mixed paint and you will find that the intensity of the colour changes. You will be able to reproduce these changes in tone by using slightly different shades of thread.

Work from the centre of the design towards the sides, always holding your arm above the paint surface to avoid smearing paint on your clothing (it will not wash out). If, after painting, the original outline has faded, or if it is likely to show through a stitched area of white or pale thread, trace over the lines with a silver water-fast pen. If you make a mistake or wish to change the colour, first allow the paint to dry, then repaint using less water in the mixture for good coverage.

Projects 7, 9 and 15 should be painted first in one or two colours. However, all the projects here can be painted onto the canvas once the waterproof pen outline is complete. This extra step takes time but makes thread selection easier, and certainly adds to the beauty of the canvas as you work on it. Learning this technique is useful for when you design your own canvas.

It is well worth adding a colour key to your canvas. At the edge of the canvas, rule a line of boxes with a waterproof pen, then fill each box with each shade of thread used in the design. You can then add the shade numbers beside each box. A minimum of 12 boxes is advisable.

CHAPTER 3
Design

Design is taking what you see and turning it into a visual poem. Drafting is looking at an object and drawing it as faithfully as possible. Design asks you to be lyrical, to show how you think and feel about a subject. Design is about *how* you perceive, not about what you perceive.

Some people are discouraged by the idea of drawing because they do not believe they have enough skill. There are many ways to overcome this. One is to photocopy a picture of the object, and then trace an outline of its main features onto transparent paper.

A second method is to abandon the draftsman's exactitude, and opt for a modern interpretation. Take the pencil in hand, relax and draw the object with one long continuous line, lifting the pencil off the paper only when you have finished.

Now add some detail. It is important to spend some time thinking and recording ideas for details such as:

- What are the dominant colours?
- Is there a border?
- Which stitches are to be used?
- Which type of thread is to be used?
- What elements still need to be drawn?

Plan the design on paper first. Once you are happy transfer it to the canvas. Do not draw on the canvas in pencil as this can stain the thread when it is stitched over. Always use a waterproof pen to ensure that the ink does not bleed into the thread, and so that the outline remains if you need to clean the canvas. If you are unsure of the ink, iron it dry, then gently dab it with a damp tissue. If it has fixed, the tissue will remain unmarked.

When you transfer the design to the canvas leave a generous border of not less than 6–7 cm. Once the design is in place under the canvas, draw in any major straight lines (for many of the designs in this book a frame is drawn first) and then trace the rest of the picture.

Colour and creating tonal areas

Colour is a deeply personal issue. Do not be uneasy about using colours that reflect emotional turmoil—if everyone were hellbent on being 'tasteful' it would be a very dull planet. The most intensely challenging art will always bend convention and bring new meanings and insights.

When selecting your coloured threads try to do it in daylight or under a lamp. Avoid purchasing thread under fluorescent light. If unavoidable, buy several variations of the colour, keep the receipt and return any unwanted shades. Another aspect of colour occurs in the way different thread textures react in light: a good comparison is velvet with its two-way nap, shiny in one direction and dull in the opposite.

All colours have tones. 'Tone' is the degree of warmth or coolness in a colour and is dependent on the intensity of the pigment, the way it absorbs light and how it mixes with or isolates the colours around it. A blend of two similar tones can result in a new colour. Harmonising colour tones share the same degree of intensity. For example, the background for the Firewheel tree in Project 6 uses dark red and deep pink to produce a dramatic dark magenta. This technique is a departure from the usual approach to shading that scatters stitches in one colour over another area of colour.

A series of harmonising tones of a similar colour can create a sense of depth in a landscape by melding areas through a gradual tonal change. This technique is also useful when only a limited amount of a desired thread is available. Blending the desired thread with one of similar tonal colour will extend its impact. Use the unstitched edge of your canvas as a palette for trying out new thread blends. This way the results can be assessed before making a final choice.

CHAPTER 4
Stretching and framing

Tools for stretching: An iron, a small spray bottle of water, a firm surface with a clean towel folded double over it, a waterproof pen, a ruler, thumbtacks, and one sheet of 10 mm foamcore that is larger than the item to be stretched.

The aim of stretching a finished canvas is to realign the weft and warp threads so they are once more at right angles to each other. The image will return to its original proportions and lose any distortion. Some canvases need more stretching than others. The lower the count number, the more force is needed to correct a twist or warp.

There are numerous ways to stretch a canvas. I use 'foamcore', a product that sandwiches a pad of lightweight foam between two sheets of cardboard. It can be cut to shape with a craft knife, can be drawn on, and is dense enough to let you slip pins into it. It comes in 3/5/10/12 mm thicknesses, of which 5 mm is the industry standard for mounting artwork. The 10 mm is useful for stretching and blocking, but if this is unavailable you can sandwich two 5 mm pieces together. Foamcore can be bought at art supply and framing shops.

Stretching your canvas

Using a waterproof pen, rule one line down and one across the middle of the foamcore sheet, creating a cross. This is a guide for straightening the canvas.

Next, mark the midpoint of each side of the canvas. Place the canvas face down on a clean towel, and with two bursts of water spray dampen lightly the back of the worked area only.

Heat an iron to wool setting, and lightly warm the back of the canvas. Do not rest the iron on one area or push it down—otherwise you will flatten the texture of the yarn. The aim is to dampen the canvas, warming and relaxing the weft and warp threads of the canvas, as well as allowing the stitching to regain some bounce.

Quickly transfer the canvas face up onto the marked foamcore. Line up the midpoints on the four sides with the cross on the foamcore. At each midpoint push a thumbtack through the canvas and into the foamcore. Work around the canvas, gently pulling it and pinning it at 1 cm intervals so that it becomes square. Allow the canvas to dry naturally out of direct sunlight. This may take two or three days, but if the weather is cold and wet it may take a few weeks. You can pull the tacks out to reposition the canvas, but avoid dampening and heating it more than once on the same day. Generally, with a large work, or one that has been damaged or distressed, stretching will be a gradual process of repeating these steps.

Once your work is dry, unpin it, hold it up to the light and examine each row for missed stitches. If you find a gap, thread a tapestry needle with a bright colour, run it through the gap and clip, leaving a 3 cm tail to mark the spot. Replace with the correct colour. Your piece is now ready for mounting and framing.

Framing

The job of a good frame is to enhance the beauty of the design and to protect the work. Framing should not be viewed as permanent as all artworks need to be cleaned, checked and restored at some time. So allow the restorer of the future enough canvas to restretch your work. Remember, too, that, many of the framing materials have a short life—staples, pins and nails corrode, adhesive tape and foam desiccate.

Unless you have the equipment and are skilled at

framing, use a professional. First decide on the colour, size and number of matt boards. The matt board goes between the edge of your canvas and the frame. Next select a frame. My framer also measures and cuts the foamcore board that fits into the back of the frame and holds my work in place. A rectangle, precisely the size of the worked canvas, is cut from the middle of the foamcore, along with a piece of wadding to pad it.

The framer can complete the rest of the work or you can follow the instructions below.

Mounting your work

Tools for framing: *Foamcore cutout, stretched canvas, waterproof pen, ruler, scissors, acid-free adhesive tape, clean towel, flat headed dressmaking pins, wadding cut to size.*

With a waterproof pen, mark the midpoints on the back of the foamcore piece the framer has cut for you. Place the canvas face down on a clean towel, then lay the wadding over it. Next put the foamcore on top, lining up the marked midpoints with the midpoints on the canvas. Pin in place on all sides at about 8 mm intervals.

Trim any excess unstitched canvas that is more than 6 cm wide. Fold the excess in towards the centre with a mitre fold in each corner, and secure with acid-free adhesive tape. The framer can now reposition the foamcore into the backing board, place the matt board on top to hide the join, and finish the framing process.

Should you use glass?

There are many arguments for avoiding glass:

- Glass is a distraction, interfering with the textures that are part of a work's appeal and limiting its sense of depth.
- It isolates the viewer from the work.
- It can squeeze and flatten the work.
- It can trap moisture.
- Non-reflective glass darkens colours and may not be aesthetically pleasing.

Glass, however, is required where a work is on public display or in a home or workplace that does not have airconditioning or central heating. Dust or airborne ash can also be a hazard. You can gently vacuum your needlework but this has a limited effect and produces wear and tear on the stitching.

If you use glass, make sure that it does not touch the surface of the work. This can be done by placing 'spacers' or thin strips of foamcore between the matt boards when two matt boards are used. The glass then rests on the second matt board, not on the stitching. Where only one matt board is used, the spacer is placed between the board and the inner edge of the frame.

Be prepared to spend on framing. Avoid a cheap alternative if a more costly frame is really more elegant and enhances your work—after all, you will look at it often. A matt board, either single or double, is essential unless the design already incorporates a border. The matt board sets the work apart from the frame and makes the work the dominating feature.

Finally, record your details on the back, as follows:

- The full name of the person who stitched it.
- Date of completion.
- Where it was made.
- Whether it celebrates a special event, e.g. birthday or anniversary
- Whether it makes a social or political statement.
- What the subject or image means to you.

Use a lead pencil as pen marks can fade, and print clearly. The more information you record, the more value and provenance it will have for future generations.

Tiny Treasure

Tent stitch, Straight stitch, French knots, Bullion knots

Tiny Treasure features a single gum blossom against a deep blue sky. It is a great first project as it is quick to make and allows the creator to try four stitches that are commonly found in other types of stitchery. It is easy to frame and the design is strong enough to hold its own amongst other artworks and pictures.

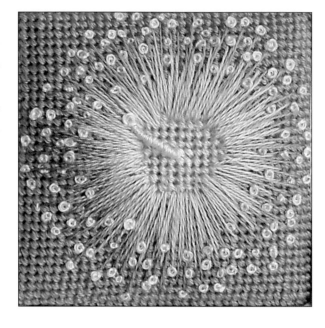

Requirements

15 x 15 cm square of white 18 count Zweigart
    interlock canvas
Waterproof pen
Ruler
No. 24 tapestry needle

Threads

Madeira Mouline 6-stranded cotton,
    1 skein of each
    0414 cerise
    0502 pale pink
    1103 dark blue
    1409 green
    2101 cream

Method

Rule a 5 cm square in the centre of the canvas, ruling along the threads of the canvas. Centre the square over the outline and trace the two circles. As they are not perfectly round, yours need not be either!

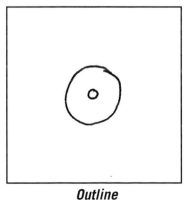

Outline

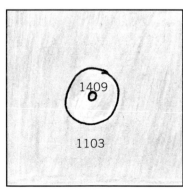

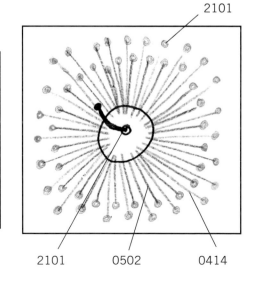

Background

With 4 strands of Mouline 1103, work in Tent stitch in horizontal rows from the top to the bottom.

Circle

First stitch the centre circle in Tent stitch with 2101, then using 1409, complete the rest of the circle.

Stamens

To complete the first layer of stamens around the flower, use a single strand of 0414. Make a small knot at one end of the thread. Anchor the thread at the back of the Tent stitch and take the needle through to the front at the edge of the green circle. Now make a series of Straight stitches of varying lengths that fan out from the edge of the green circle. Repeat, this time using a single strand of 0502, and make the Straight stitches shorter but still of varying lengths.

Using a single strand of 2101, scatter French knots at the ends of most of the stamens as well as a few on the blue background.

Style

This protrudes from the cream flower centre. Make a Bullion knot of 15–20 wraps with a single strand of Mouline 2101, and place a French knot at its end.

Twining Gum Leaves

Tent stitch, Long stitch

T his simple yet elegant project can be completed in a weekend. There is no need to stay with the colours selected here. Your leaves might be a collection of strong, bright hues with a deep blue sky behind. A design as simple as this gives you the freedom to choose fresh colours every time you stitch it. A double mount will show off this work to best effect.

Requirements

22 x 15 cm of white 18 count Zweigart interlock
   canvas
Waterproof pen
Ruler
No. 24 tapestry needle

Threads

Cascade House Mohair: 1 skein of each
      except for 1520.
      1520 yellow, 2 skeins*
      1760 khaki
      1780 light green
      2350 tan
      3050 apricot
      7570 olive
      7590 leaf green
*   If using another brand, ensure that you have at
      least 11 metres

Method

Centre the outline under the canvas and rule a border of 4 cm x 12 cm, using the threads of the canvas as a guide. Trace the rest of the design.

Background

Work in Tent stitch using a single strand of 1520 mohair. Note: because mohair is more delicate than sheep's wool or cotton, it is important to sew with shorter lengths of thread. Stitch in horizontal rows, moving from top to bottom.

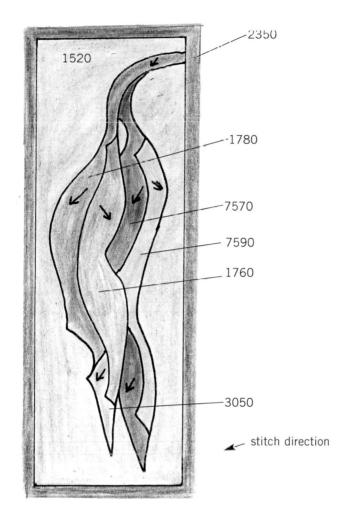

2350

1520

1780

7570

7590

1760

3050

← stitch direction

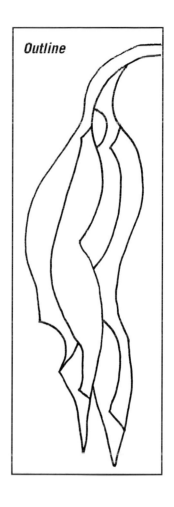

Outline

Outer border

Work three rows of Tent stitch in 2350 around the background to make a frame for the picture.

Front leaf

In 1780, start at the top of the stalk and work down the left side of the leaf in diagonal Long stitch, sloping the same way as the Tent stitch and stopping before the tip where the colour changes to 3050 (pink). Stitch this pink section in Long stitch ending with Tent stitch at the very tip. In 1760, work the right side of the leaf from top to bottom in diagonal Long stitch with the slope going in the opposite direction to that of the left side.

Rear leaf

In 7570, start at the top of the stalk and stitch down the left side in diagonal Long stitch, sloping the same way as the Tent stitch. Then change to Tent stitch and work the left-hand tip. Next, in 7590, work the right side of the leaf from top to bottom in diagonal Long stitch, sloping in the opposite direction to that of the left side.

Dancing Flowers

Tent stitch, French knots

This design could be used in a variety of ways—for example, as a panel for an evening bag, a motif for the lid of a box, or enlarged on a photocopier and worked on a 10-count canvas for a comfortable sofa cushion. It is an ideal project for a beginner in needlepoint since it has a simple form and colour range. The inspiration for this design comes from the small native irises and delicate orchids that are easily overlooked in the bush.

Requirements

30 cm x 30 cm square of white 18 count
    Zweigart interlock canvas
Waterproof pen
Ruler
No. 24 tapestry needle

Threads

Note: If you choose this design for something other than a framed artwork, use durable threads such as cotton or wool instead of silk.

DMC Medicis Wool
    8173 apricot, 3 skeins
    8341 light lime green, 1 skein
    8342 lime green, 1 skein
Cascade House Lame Silk, 1 card of each
    1000 white
    1340 cream
    2135 yellow
    9540 dark blue
Cascade House Pearl Silk, 2 cards
    8900 pale blue

Method

Centre the outline under the canvas and rule the border, then trace the rest of the design.

Background

Work in Tent stitch using 2 threads of Medicis Wool 8173. Stitch in horizontal rows from the top to the bottom.

Leaves

In Tent stitch work the leaf vein first in 2 threads of 8341, then the leaf body in 2 threads of 8342.

Flowers

Work in Tent stitch using a single thread. First stitch the centres of the large flowers in Lame 1340, then the pale blue petals in Pearl Silk 8900. Next, stitch the small flower centres in Lame 2135, then the dark blue petals in Lame 9540.

Outline

French knots

Work these last of all. Make them in Lame Silk 1000 with a double wrap of thread around the needle and sit them on the surface of the Tent stitches.

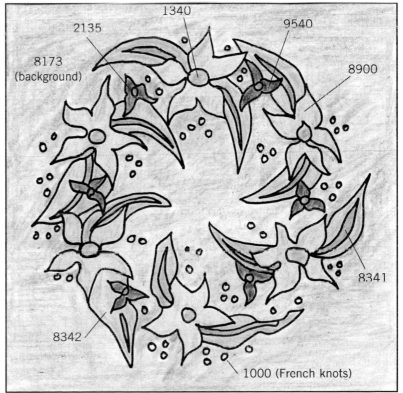

2135
1340
9540
8173
(background)
8900
8341
8342
1000 (French knots)

Silk and Gold Telopea

Tent stitch

There are times when you deserve utter luxury. Silk is a delightful fibre to sew with because of its soft and shiny look and the way it slithers through the canvas. The colours are rich and yet not overpowering. This work is for the most sumptuous corner of your home.

Requirements

30 cm x 30 cm square of white 18 count Zweigart
　　interlock canvas
Waterproof pen
No. 24 tapestry needle
A small block of beeswax if Kreinik braid is
　　unavailable

Threads

Note: silk should be cut in shorter lengths than
　　wool because it quickly wears thin with use.
Gumnut Yarns Silk Buds, 1 skein of each
　　except for 406

075 light plum	628 dark gumleaf green
198 dark plum	679 khaki
406 light blue, 2 skeins	823 light pink
563 light gumleaf green	825 medium pink
569 dark green	829 red

Kreinik Gold Metallic Balger Medium, 1 reel
　　#16 gold braid

Method

Centre the outline under the canvas and rule each side of the design, following the weft and warp threads of the canvas. Then trace the rest of the design. A light pen outline should be sufficient.

To prevent the delicate silk thread from catching and wearing out on the rough edge of the canvas, sew a ribbon binding around the canvas edge.

Tent stitch is used throughout.

For each thread use as a single thread in the needle. Kreinik braid is preferred, as it does not unravel. However, if you use a substitute thread and it starts to untwist, pull the ends of the thread over the edge of a block of beeswax so they adhere to each other.

Background

Work Tent stitch in horizontal rows, from top to bottom. Stitch the Kreinik metallic thread first, then the light blue background with Gumnut Silk Buds 406.

Waratah leaves

Stitch each leaf vein before completing the rest of the leaf. Note that the top pair of leaves are in different shades of green (563, 628) from the bottom pair of leaves (569, 679).

Waratah flower

Stitch the flower centre first with 825, then the stamens with 829. For the rest of the flower stitch the darkest shade 198 first, then 075 and finally 823.

The White Waratah

Tent stitch, French knots, thread blending

Ihnh spite of the heartache this design caused, it is still a favourite. It is a calm and restful image, with delicate tones of blended threads. These flowers are like sisters as they embrace and support each other. White waratahs are rare. The few that I have seen have much darker leaves and the plants and flowers are smaller than their red counterparts. The red waratah can withstand brighter light and so, perhaps, a wider range of habitat.

Requirements

30 cm x 30 cm square of white 18 count
 Zweigart interlock canvas
Waterproof pen
No. 24 tapestry needle

Threads

DMC Medicis Wool, 1 skein of each unless stated
 otherwise
 Blanc white
 Ecru off-white
 8328 cream
 8369 pale eucalypt green
 8404 deep green
 8406 eucalypt green, 2 skeins
 8407 seaweed
 8417 green
 8419 verdant green
 8426 blue-grey, 2 skeins

Method

Centre the outline under the canvas and rule up the square, taking care to rule along the tops of the threads. Lightly trace the outline of the design.

Tent stitch is used throughout, in 2 threads of wool. The French knots are worked in the flower centres last of all.

Flowers

Work in Tent stitch and follow the colour chart for the sepal thread colours. Where the edges of the sepals touch, blend 1 thread of Blanc with 1 thread of 8419.

Top flower

To work the sepals, alternate Ecru with 8328. Stitch the inner centre with 8328, then the outer centre in Blanc. Stitch in Ecru the area that joins the centre to the sepals.

Ecru

8328

8419 + Blanc
(outline stitch)

8426

8406

8404 and
8417

8404

8407 and
8417

Blanc

8417 (veins &
leaf outline)

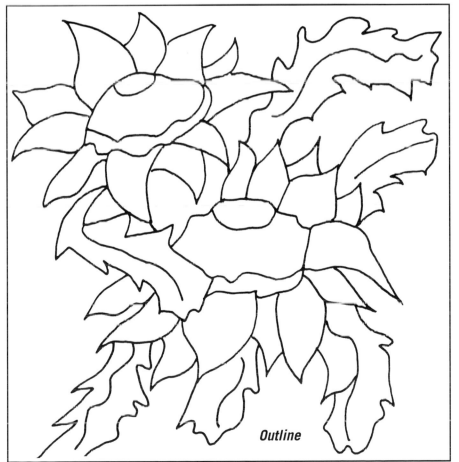

Outline

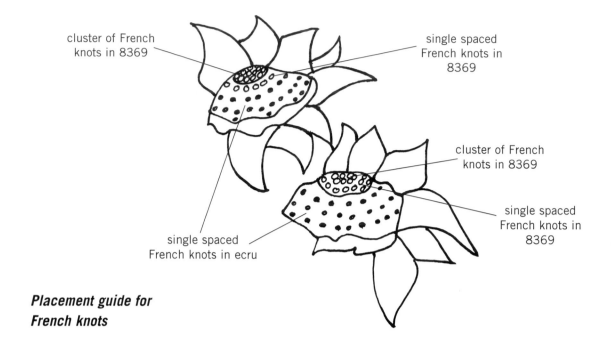

cluster of French knots in 8369

single spaced French knots in 8369

cluster of French knots in 8369

single spaced French knots in 8369

single spaced French knots in ecru

Placement guide for French knots

Lower flower

Work the sepals in Blanc. Tent stitch the outline, blending 1 thread each of Blanc and 8419. Work the inner centre in 8328, then the outer centre in Blanc. For the area that joins the centre to the sepals, use 8328.

Flower centres

French knots are placed in the centres of both flowers as shown on the placement guide. For each knot use a single wrap of thread around the needle. (Refer to Chapter 2 for French knots).

Leaves

With 8417, in Tent stitch over each leaf's pen outline, then over its vein. Next stitch the body of the leaves according to the colours on the chart. Note that some of the leaf areas require a blend of two different colours.

Border and background

For the border work 10 rows of Tent stitch in 8406, starting from the outer edges and working in from all sides. The centre background area is worked in 8426.

The Firewheel Tree

Tent stitch, thread blending

S tenocarpus sinuatus, the firewheel tree, is a hardy rainforest tree that flowers in late summer. Its flowers are like spokes on a wheel, often tangling with each other to produce drifts of raucous red and orange blossom. This design is a stylised interpretation that preserves the highly individual character of each flower on the wheel.

Requirements

30 x 30 cm square of white 18 count
   Zweigart interlock canvas
Waterproof pen
Ruler
No. 24 tapestry needle

Threads

DMC Medicis Wool

   8127 red, 1 skein
   8212 grape, 2 skeins
   8305 fawn, 1 skein
   8413 leaf green, 1 skein
   8417 green, 2 skeins
   8419 verdant green, 1 skein
   8500 charcoal, 1 skein
   8685 magenta, 2 skeins
   8940 bright orange, 1 skein
   8941 orange, 1 skein

Method

Centre the outline underneath the canvas. Draw the square first, ruling along the threads of the canvas, then draw the design with a waterproof pen. Use Tent stitch throughout.

Flowers

Work with 2 threads of Medicis wool in Tent stitch. First, work the three red flowerheads of the central firewheel in 8127, then change to 8940 for the flowerhead tips. This colour sequence is reversed for the orange flowerheads: work them in 8940, then the tips in 8127. Likewise, use 8940 then 8127 for the partial firewheel flowers on the upper and lower left-hand side of the design. Finally, work the two green firewheel centres in 8413, then all the tendrils, also in 8413. In 8941 work the flower stalks that join the flowerheads to the flower centres (see colour chart).

Leaf

Tent stitch the veins in 8305. Then, following the colour chart, work the upperside of the leaf in 8417 and the underside in 8419.

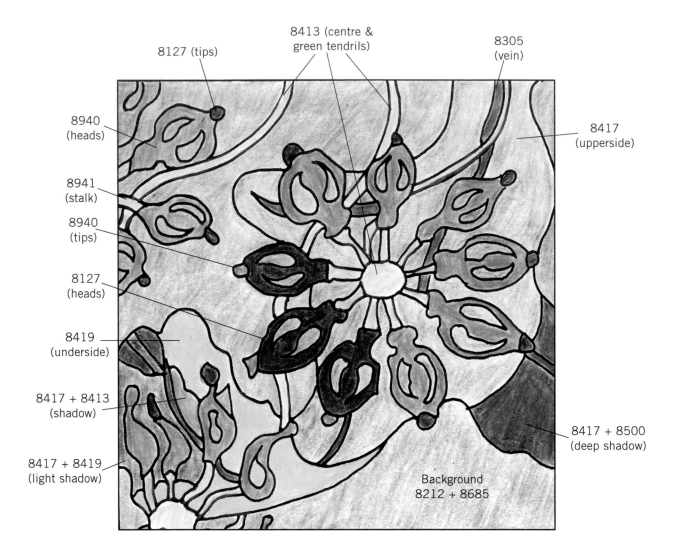

8127 (tips)

8413 (centre & green tendrils)

8305 (vein)

8940 (heads)

8941 (stalk)

8940 (tips)

8127 (heads)

8419 (underside)

8417 + 8413 (shadow)

8417 + 8419 (light shadow)

8417 (upperside)

8417 + 8500 (deep shadow)

Background 8212 + 8685

Leaf shadows

For the three leaf shadows, refer to the colour chart and blend 1 strand of each colour as follows.

Deep shadow

Blend 8417 and 8500 for the far right-hand side of the leaf, and for the underside of the tip on either side of the central vein.

Shadow

Blend 8417 and 8413 for the small area on the right-hand side of the central vein on the underside of the leaf.

Light shadow

Blend 8417 and 8419 for the left-hand side of the central vein on the underside of the leaf.

Background

For the rich magenta background, blend 1 thread of 8212 and 1 thread of 8685. Work in horizontal rows from top to bottom, in Tent stitch.

Outline

Gondwanaland

Tent stitch, Long stitch, French knots (optional), thread blending (optional), painting

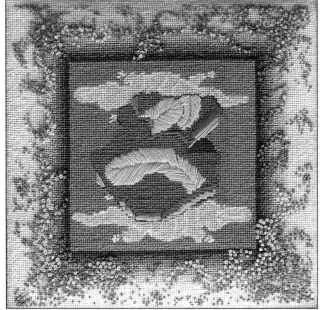

This design is like a timeline. The three Glossopteris leaf fossils date back to 280–225 million years ago, when Australia was part of Gondwanaland. Two crocodiles swim behind the stone symbolising the power of the Dreamtime, held in an ancient oral form and passed down in myth and law by the Aboriginal nation.

Around this image is a border of warm red-orange. This symbolizes the land as it is today, dry and desiccated with scattered saltbush and grasses.

Note: two versions of the border are offered: a simple 11-row border in a single colour; and a saltbush border involving thread blending and hundreds of French knots (for addicts only!).

Requirements

30 x 30 cm white square of 18 count mono canvas
Waterproof pen
Ruler
Jo Sonja's Textile Medium
Jo Sonja's acrylic paint: brilliant violet and cobalt
   blue
Paintbrush
White towel
No. 24 tapestry needle

Threads

DMC Medicis wool, 1 skein of each
Gondwanaland and single colour border
   Noir black
   8128 ochre (2 skeins)

8208 storm
8210 pale grey-blue
8331 violet grey
8333 jacaranda blue
8397 pale violet
8794 purple
8800 pale sea blue
8895 violet

Additional threads for saltbush border
   8113 blush
   8129 mid tangerine
   8139 pale tangerine
   8303 wet sand
   8402 olive green
   8420 pale green
   8515 oatmeal
   8799 sky blue

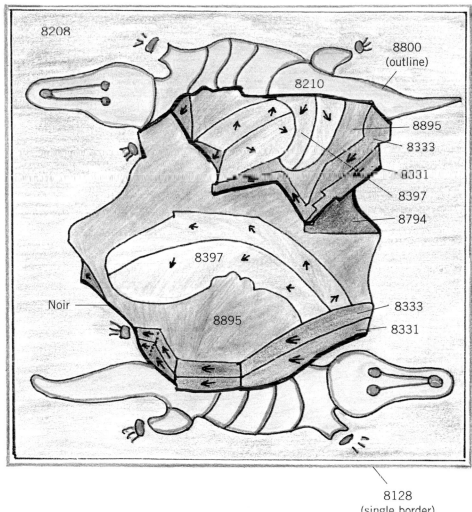

8208
8800 (outline)
8210
8895
8333
8331
8397
8794
Noir
8397
8895
8333
8331

8128
(single border)

Method

Centre the outline under the canvas and trace the design with a waterproof pen. Painting the design with a light wash of colour is advisable to prevent the white canvas from showing through the Long stitch. Refer to Chapter 3 for techniques.

To paint the fossil (the three leaf prints in stone), mix 5 mL of water with a pea-sized amount of brilliant violet acrylic and a drop of the textile medium. For the background and crocodiles, mix the same amounts of water, medium and acrylic but this time use cobalt blue. Avoid painting over the pen outline.

Make sure the canvas is dry before stitching. Work all stitches with 2 strands of Medicis Wool.

Fossil

Follow the colour chart. First, work the stone areas of 8895 (main colour) and 8794, in Tent stitch. Next, work top stone layer in 8333 and bottom stone layer (deep shade) in 8331, both in Long stitch.

The leaf imprints, in 8397, are worked in Long stitch that gradually changes direction (follow the arrows on the chart) to enhance their shape.

To outline the stone and main fracture plane, work a single thread of Noir in small Straight stitches. This frees the stone from its background and lets it float above the crocodiles as though adrift through time.

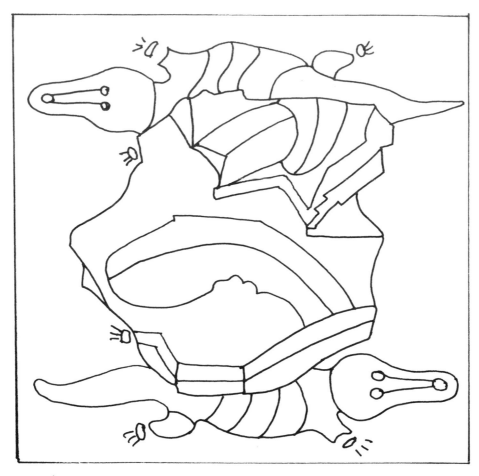

Outline

Crocodiles

Outline each crocodile and stitch the lines across their bodies in 8800. For the crocodile bodies use 8210. All are worked in Tent stitch.

Background

Work in Tent stitch in 8208.

Border

Single-colour border

Work in Tent stitch to make an 11-row red ochre desert surround in 8128.

Saltbush border

Work in Tent stitch. Start from the sides of the central design and work outwards to the edge of the canvas, as follows:

Rows 1 and 2	8128, 2 threads
Rows 3 and 4	8128 + 8129 (1 thread of each)
Rows 5 and 6	8129, 2 threads
Rows 7 and 8	8129 + 8113 (1 thread of each)
Rows 9 and 10	8113, 2 threads
Rows 11 and 12	8113 + 8139 (1 thread of each)
Rows 13 to 23	8139, 2 threads
Rows 24 to 28	8799, 2 threads
Row 29	8515 + 8303 (1 thread of each)
Rows 30 and 31	8303 (1 thread of each)

The swathes of saltbush and native groundcovers are made with single-wrap French knots in the following order: 8402 olive green; 8420 pale green; 8799 sky blue; and 8303 wet sand. Place them wherever you wish, or use the photo of the finished work as a guide.

Toute Petite

Straight stitch, Tent stitch, thread blending

T his design is based on three tiny ceramic jars that are part of a small and greatly loved collection. Their bright cheerful colours and touches of gold are a celebration of spring, and reflect the delights of sunny days without summer's overbearing heat. Delicate objects that are greatly loved, yet not suitable for daily use are often ideal subjects for a needlepoint. Your own interpretation of them will mean they can be admired all the more!

Requirements

32 x 30 cm of white 18 count Zweigart
   interlock canvas
Waterproof pen
Ruler
No. 24 tapestry needle
A small block of beeswax

Threads

DMC Stranded Cotton, 1 skein of each
   Blanc white
   208 violet
   727 yellow
   906 bright green
   907 lime green
   962 pink
   963 pale pink
   995 ocean blue
   996 sky blue
   3845 aqua blue

DMC Medicis Wool, 1 skein of each
   Ecru off-white
   8328 cream
Madeira Silk, 4 skeins of each
   112 cream
   305 apricot
Madeira Metallic No. 4
   4007 yellow gold, 1 skein

Method

Cut out a 32 x 30 cm piece of white 18 count canvas. Centre the outline underneath and with a waterproof pen copy it lightly on to the canvas, beginning with the straight sides of the outer box and following a single thread of the canvas for each straight line. Draw the sides of the inner box. Trace the curves with a single flowing line. It is not necessary to create a symmetrical form for any of the jars.

Jars

Each jar is worked in Tent stitch. Work the areas of gold first. Use it unsplit but pass the end of the thread over the beeswax before threading the needle. This helps to control the cut ends, which tend to fray apart.

Using gold thread, Tent stitch the golden bands on the jars, the pointed lid tops and, with the two smaller jars, the base. With the largest jar, gold thread is Tent stitched around the flower centre and along the lines that radiate out to the petal edge. An outline in Straight stitch using 2 strands of gold thread is stitched after all the other areas of the jar are complete. Note that all areas of DMC stranded cotton are stitched with 4 strands of thread.

Left-hand jar

Tent stitch the yellow flower centres in DMC cotton 727, then the pink petals in 962 and 963. Outline both with small Straight stitches in 2 strands of gold thread.

Centre jar

Following the chart, work these colours first, in Tent stitch: DMC stranded cotton 727 yellow, 907 lime green, 962 pink, 963 pale pink, 996 sky blue, and 3845 aqua blue.

Then fill in with DMC cotton 208 violet, the main colour. Outline the flower centres and petal edges with 2 strands of gold thread in small Straight stitches.

Right-hand jar

Tent stitch the coloured areas first in DMC cotton 962, 906 and 907 before stitching in white. Then Tent stitch in 4007 the gold lines at the base of the jar.

Background

Behind the jars is a square of creamy yellow Tent stitch that mimics the texture of silk fabric. To create this special effect combine 1 strand of Medicis Wool 8328 with 3 strands of Madeira Silk

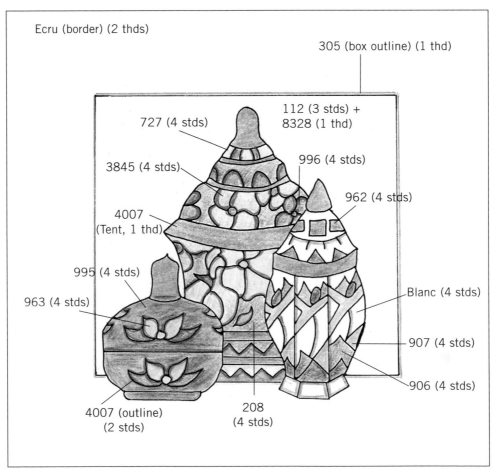

Ecru (border) (2 thds)

305 (box outline) (1 thd)

727 (4 stds)

112 (3 stds) + 8328 (1 thd)

3845 (4 stds)

996 (4 stds)

4007 (Tent, 1 thd)

962 (4 stds)

995 (4 stds)

963 (4 stds)

Blanc (4 stds)

907 (4 stds)

906 (4 stds)

4007 (outline) (2 stds)

208 (4 stds)

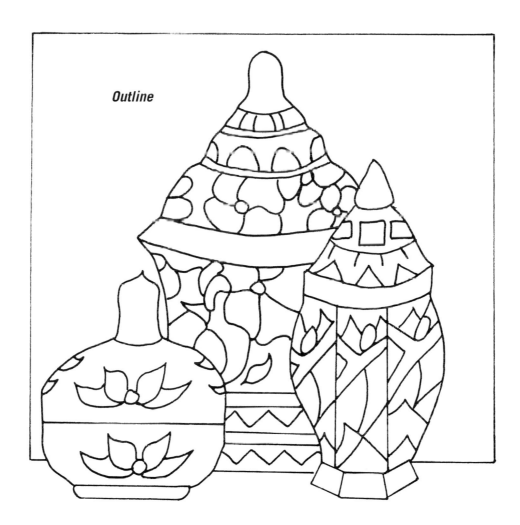

Outline

112 in the same needle. Next, outline the square with a single row of Madeira 305; this thread is used unsplit.

Border

A framework of simple Tent stitch sets off the jars with a woven bamboo screen effect. A double strand of Ecru Medicis Wool in the needle makes this a fast, easy background method.

All the rows are worked from top to bottom, starting on the left-hand side and working along the top of the outer box. Fill in this area by following the pattern from left to right as follows:

Vertical row 1
Tent stitch the first stitch, miss the second, Tent stitch the third stitch, and continue working this way, missing every alternate stitch until the row is complete.

Vertical row 2
Leave it unworked.

Vertical row 3
Work a line of Tent stitches, missing every second stitch BUT start one horizontal canvas thread lower than the stitch on the first row to build a diagonal movement into the pattern.

Vertical row 4
Leave it unworked.

Repeat Rows 1 to 4, then work last row of Tent stitch to enclose the design.

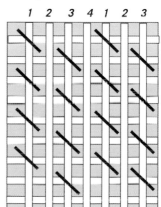

Bacchus

Tent stitch, painting, counted chart supplied

This design has evolved over several redraws and two very different versions. The original inspiration was a terracotta mask, and the memories of an early morning stroll from the peaceful greenery of the amphitheatre to the heart of the Pompeii Scavi. The terracotta head is of a youthful Bacchus, the Roman god of wine and theatre (the Greek god Dionysus renamed). It borrows a colour palette typical of the small painted wall medallions that decorated the houses of wealthy citizens.

Requirements

30 x 30 cm square of 18 count Zweigart interlock canvas
Waterproof pen
Jo Sonja's acrylic paint: green oxide
Jo Sonja's Textile Medium
Paintbrush
White towel
No. 24 tapestry needle

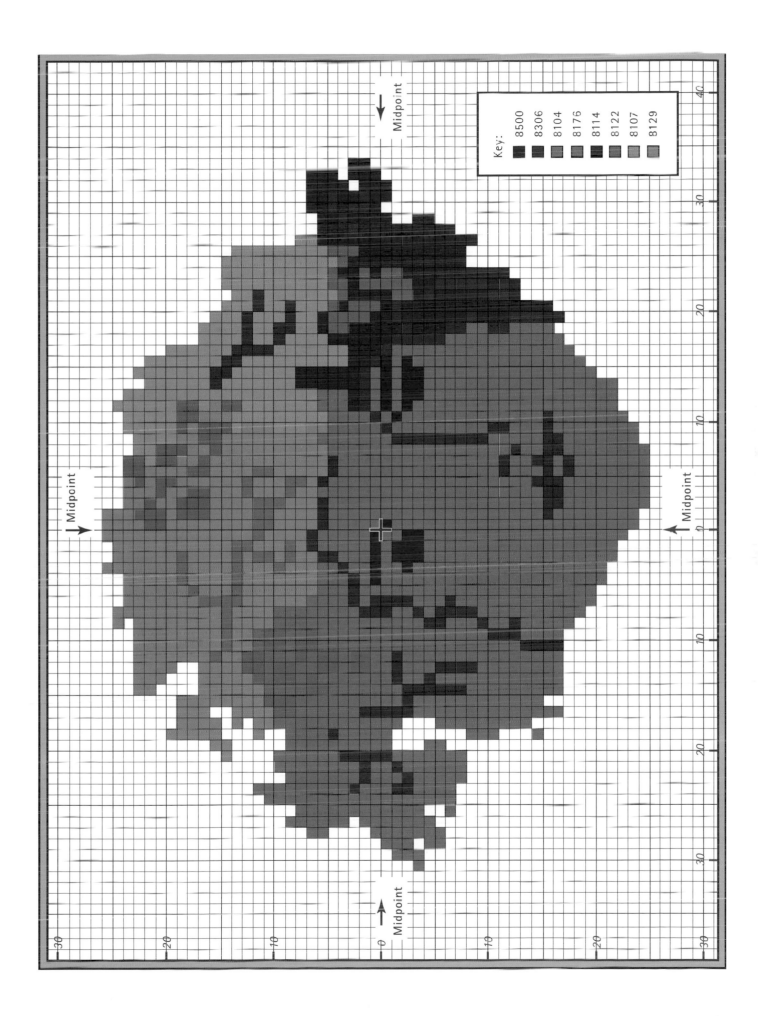

Midpoint

Midpoint

Midpoint

Midpoint

Key: 8500 8306 8104 8176 8114 8122 8107 8129

Threads

DMC Medicis Wool, 1 skein of each

  8104 russet
  8107 latte
  8114 rust
  8122 dark plum
  8129 mid tangerine
  8176 cedar
  8306 dark brown
  8500 charcoal
  3 skeins of 8409 dark green for the background

Method

Centre the canvas over the outline and trace a 13 cm circle onto the canvas with care as this marks the edge of the background stitching.

Paint

Put a light green wash over the circle with a pea-sized amount of green oxide mixed with 5 mL of water and a drop of textile medium. (Refer to Chapter 3 for more about painting.) Allow the canvas to dry before starting to stitch.

Preparation for stitching

Find the midpoint of your circle on the canvas by folding the circle in half both ways and marking the midpoint with a small dot: this corresponds to the midpoint on the chart where the lines marked 0 meet. Start the first stitch here.

Face

Following the counted chart, stitch with a double thread in Tent stitch.

Background

Stitch with a double thread of 8409 in Tent stitch. Work in horizontal rows from top to bottom. Stitching should cover the traced circle.

Flannel Flowers

Tent stitch, Wheat stitch, Long stitch, French knots, thread blending

F lannel flowers (*Actinotis helianthi*) are found along the coast in sandy soils which remain damp and cool in the crevices of the sandstone outcrops. Buffeted by strong sea breezes, they have evolved a soft furry exterior to minimise water loss through their leaf pores, and a luminous silver green-grey foliage colour to withstand the harsh glare of the sun. They have adapted to a bushfire ecology and germinate after a burn, flowering well in the following spring and summer.

Requirements

30 x 30 cm square of white 18 count Zweigart
   interlock canvas
Waterproof pen
Ruler
No 24 tapestry needle

Threads

DMC Medicis Wool, 1 skein of each
   except for 8739

Blanc white	8407 seaweed
Ecru off-white	8421 whitish green
Noir black	8426 blue-grey
8204 dark grey-green	8427 pale blue
8305 fawn	8515 oatmeal
8306 dark brown	8739 putty, 2 skeins
8320 chestnut	8798 mid sea blue
8341 light lime green	8800 pale sea blue
8344 tropical green	8871 green mist
8346 grass green	8898 clover green
8403 dark olive green	8899 deep sea blue
8406 eucalypt green	8904 bright green

DMC Stranded Cotton, 1 skein
   3046 golden green
DMC Metallic, 1 skein
   5282 gold
Gumnut Yarns Silk Buds, 1 skein
   406 light blue

Method

Centre the outline under the canvas and rule the border, leaving breaks in the line at the lower left section for the flower petals that overhang it. Trace the rest of the design onto the canvas.

Chart 1: Landscape

Follow Chart 1 for thread placement. The sky, ocean, surf, headland and beach are all worked in Tent stitch. Use one thread of Silk Buds 406 for the sky. For the headland use a double thread of Medicis Wool 8320. The ocean, surf, rocks and headland shadows are a blend of one thread of

Chart 1: Landscape

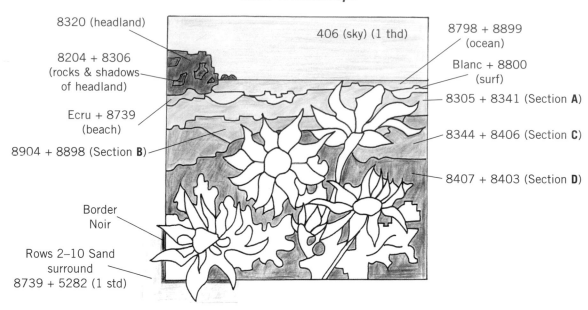

8320 (headland)

8204 + 8306 (rocks & shadows of headland)

Ecru + 8739 (beach)

8904 + 8898 (Section **B**)

Border Noir

Rows 2–10 Sand surround 8739 + 5282 (1 std)

406 (sky) (1 thd)

8798 + 8899 (ocean)

Blanc + 8800 (surf)

8305 + 8341 (Section **A**)

8344 + 8406 (Section **C**)

8407 + 8403 (Section **D**)

each colour as indicated.

The background to the flannel flowers changes colour through a series of thread blends. Section **A** blends 8305 and 8341; **B** blends 8904 and 8898; **C** blends 8344 and 8406; **D** blends 8407 and 8403. Sections **A**, **B**, and **C** are all in Tent stitch, and Section **D** is in Wheat stitch (see Chapter 2).

Chart 2: Flannel flowers

The instructions for the flannel flowers include the grey-green leaves. Stitch with 2 threads of Medicis Wool in a single colour or blend two colours.

Flower 1

Leaves: Tent stitch over the leaf outline in 8427, then fill in the body of the leaves with 8426.
Flower petals: Tent stitch with 8426, working 1–3 stitches on the tips of the three petals that extend over the sand surround. The uppermost petal has 1 stitch, the next has 2 and the lowest has 3 stitches. Where the petals share an edge, stitch a single row of 8871. Work the shaded area of the petal centres in 8515. Stitch the remaining petal areas with Blanc.
Flower centre: Tent stitch with 8421. Make single-wrap French knots using 1 strand of DMC stranded cotton 3046; refer to Chart 2 for their placement.

Flower 2

Leaves: Tent stitch over their outlines in 8427, then fill in the rest of the leaves with 8204.
Flower petals: Tent stitch the tip of the lowest petal with 2 stitches of 8426. Where the edges of the petals touch, stitch with a single line of 8871. Complete the remaining petal area in Blanc.
Flower centre: Tent stitch with 8421, then work single-wrap French knots in 1 strand of DMC cotton 3046 as indicated on the flower chart.

Flower 3

Stem: Stitch in Tent stitch with 8341.
Petals: Use 8871 in a single line of Tent stitch to mark where the petals meet. Stitch the narrowest petal in Blanc, then complete the rest of the petal area with a blend of 1 thread of 8421 and 1 of Ecru.
Buds: Work these in Long stitch, following the direction arrows on the chart, in 8341.

Flower 4

Leaves: Tent stitch over each leaf outline and vein on the lower right side in 8427, then fill in the body of the leaves with 8426.
Stem: Work in Tent stitch with 8341.

Chart 2: Flannel flowers

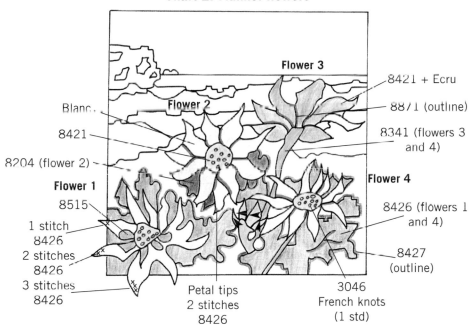

Flower: With 8871 work a single row of Tent stitch to mark the line where the petals touch. Tent stitch the rest of the petal area in Blanc.

Flower centre: Tent stitch in 8421. Work single wrap French knots in 1 strand of 3046; refer to Chart 2 for placement.

Border

Stitch a single row of Tent stitch in Noir over the outline of the square border.

Sand surround

Tent stitch all sides of the picture, as follows:

Row 1: Blend 2 threads of 8739 and 1 strand of DMC Metallic 5282.

Row 2: Work in 2 threads of 8739.

Repeat these two rows four times.

Enlarge outline to 133% on a photocopier

Dawn

Tent stitch, Long stitch, Straight stitch, French knots

It is spring at last, after a hard dry winter. The old curled leaves display reds, mottled pinks and purples, yellows and faded greens, all cross-hatched with trails of insect attack. They hang raggedly and sigh gently against each other until it is time to fall. Their life as uniform grey-green leaves has been exchanged for a triumph of bold colour, texture and shape.

Requirements

20 x 25 cm white 18 count Zweigart interlock
    canvas
Waterproof pen
Ruler
No. 24 tapestry needle

Threads

This design was created for hand-dyed yarns. Fibres such as mohair, silk, cotton, and fine wool (1-ply or 2-ply) may be used. The idea is to choose a collection of threads that harmonise in tone. For this to work well it is wise to view your threads together prior to purchase. Since aqua is the dominant tone, all the other threads should harmonise with whichever shade of aqua you choose.

The mohair wool used in Dawn is a gorgeous thread with a very high lustre. As the process of hand dyeing often produces quite marked variations between dye lots, an exact match may be impossible. If you can buy the mohair from Littlewood Fleece Yarns (at the 'A Frame' shop in Euroa, Victoria) you will need the following—there are no numbers, only names.

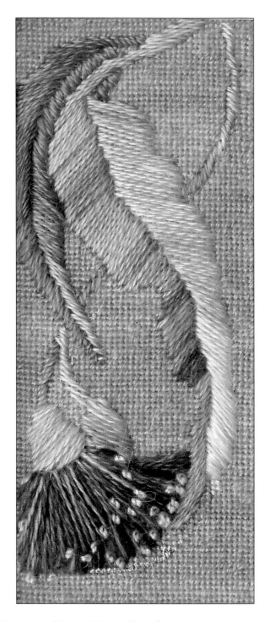

Littlewood Fleece Yarns Mohair

1 hank each of bright yellow, pale yellow, orange, brown orange, buttercup, mustard, shocking pink, rainbow, red rainbow, green, light green, pine green, 3 hanks of aqua

DMC Metallic 5282 gold, 1 skein

Method

Centre the outline underneath the canvas and lightly trace the rectangle, ruling along the threads of the canvas. Check the position of the outline and trace the rest of the design.

Background

Work the background first, in Tent stitch with a single strand of aqua in the needle. Remember to keep your thread short if you are using mohair or silk as these delicate threads wear quickly.

Large leaf

First, Tent stitch the tip, blending 1 thread of orange with 2 strands of DMC Metallic 5282 gold.

Then, starting at the top of the leaf stalk, work in diagonal Long stitch down to the tip. Follow the chart for colour placement and stitch direction (see arrows). The thread for each colour change can be anchored in the back of the Tent-stitched area running alongside. Avoid pulling the thread tight, and repeat the stitch if thread coverage is thin. Where the stitch direction changes, a couple of stitches will fan out from the same hole.

Small leaf

Work in diagonal Long stitch, following the chart for colour and stitch direction.

Flowers

Flower stalk and cup

Follow the arrows on the chart and work small diagonal Long stitches in rainbow.

Flower 2

This is stitched first because it hangs behind Flower 1. Straight stitches in red rainbow fan out to the lower left side of the large leaf.

Flower 1

Work long and short Straight Stitches, in shocking pink, so that it appears to hang in front.

Outline

Stamens

Place single-wrap French knots randomly along the edge of the flowers: in pale yellow for Flower 1, bright yellow for Flower 2.

Framing

A clean and careful framer is essential, as this thread is delicate and will fluff with prolonged handling. It is advisable to use glass with spacers between double mount boards to protect the work and to preserve the lustre of the mohair wool.

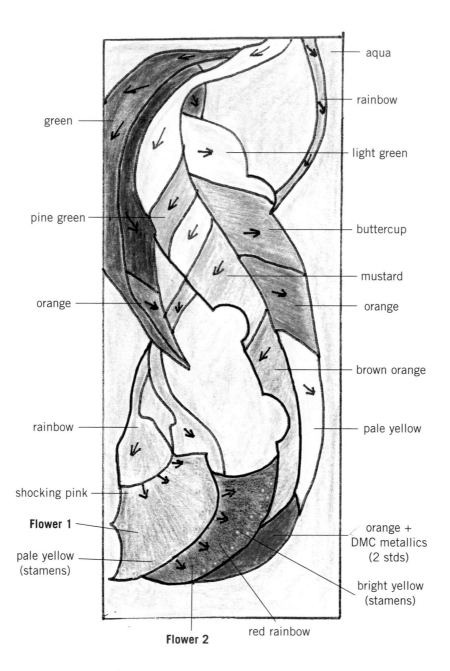

aqua

rainbow

green

light green

pine green

buttercup

mustard

orange

orange

brown orange

rainbow

pale yellow

shocking pink

Flower 1

pale yellow
(stamens)

orange +
DMC metallics
(2 stds)

bright yellow
(stamens)

Flower 2

red rainbow

Stitch direction ⟋

Misty Mountains

Tent stitch, Straight stitch, Wheat stitch, French knots, thread blending

The foreground shows windblown tufted grasses and those small trees that cling to a cliff edge with iron roots. Below is the mist, a rolling cloud, which flows around the lesser peaks and makes them islands, occasionally thinning to reveal the valley floor below. The dark peaks in the distance are in silhouette, becoming shadowy towards the horizon until they finally melt into the grey sky above. Far off a scrap of blue shows fine weather ahead.

Requirements
20 cm x 33 cm rectangle of white 18 count
　　Zweigart interlock canvas
Waterproof pen
Ruler
No. 24 tapestry needle

Threads
DMC Medicis Wool, 1 skein of each
　　except for 8415

Ecru off-white
8204 dark grey-green
8214 mist
8313 sandstone
8328 cream
8381 pale grey
8403 dark olive green
8405 pale olive green
8408 dark eucalypt green
8411 misty light grey
8415 forest green, 2 skeins
8416 blackforest green
8742 pale orange
8800 pale sea blue
8877 grey
8996 deep azure blue
8997 azure blue
Madeira Silk, 1 skein of each
　　1409 light green
　　1603 mid green
　　1803 grey
Kaalund 2-Ply Wool, 1 skein
　　2468 variegated forest green

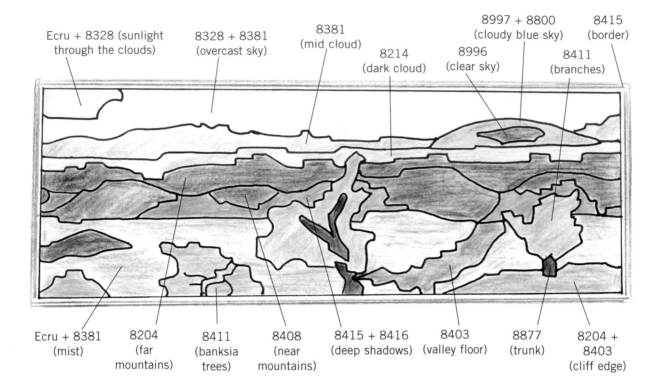

Ecru + 8328 (sunlight through the clouds)
8328 + 8381 (overcast sky)
8381 (mid cloud)
8214 (dark cloud)
8997 + 8800 (cloudy blue sky)
8996 (clear sky)
8411 (branches)
8415 (border)

Ecru + 8381 (mist)
8204 (far mountains)
8411 (banksia trees)
8408 (near mountains)
8415 + 8416 (deep shadows)
8403 (valley floor)
8877 (trunk)
8204 + 8403 (cliff edge)

Method

Centre the design under the canvas and rule the sides of the rectangle first, following the threads of the canvas as a guide. Copy the rest of the design.

Sky

Stitch in Tent stitch with a double thread in the needle. Where 2 thread numbers are given together, blend 1 thread of each shade. Work each section in neat horizontal rows from the top to the bottom of the design.

Mountains

Continue as before with Tent stitch, blending 1 thread of each shade where 2 thread colours are recorded.

Valley

Stitch the mist's colour blend of Ecru and 8381 pale grey, in Tent stitch, then the valley floor in 8403 dark olive green. Stitch the small island of green standing out from the mist on the left-hand side in 8408 dark eucalypt green.

Cliff edge

Tent stitch a blend of 8204 dark grey-green and 8403 dark olive green.

Banksia trees

Tent stitch the branches of the banksia on the left-hand side with 8411 misty light grey, then the trunks of the banksia trees at the centre and right-hand side of the design in 8877 grey. Tent stitch all the banksia foliage in 2 strands of Kaalund 2468 variegated forest green.

Border

Stitch 2 rows of 8415 forest green around the design in Tent stitch.

Raised stitches

Follow the Raised Stitches Chart
Left side
Use a single strand of Madeira Silk 1803 grey in Wheat stitch to mimic branches on the small island of green. Then make small clusters of single-wrap French knots for the tops of the gum trees, using a

Left side

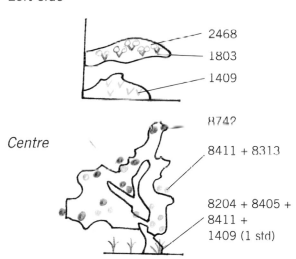

2468
1803
1409

Centre

8742
8411 + 8313

8204 + 8405 +
8411 +
1409 (1 std)

Valley

2468

2468

Right side

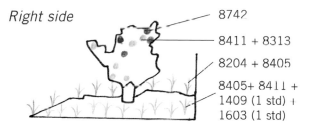

8742
8411 + 8313
8204 + 8405
8405+ 8411 +
1409 (1 std) +
1603 (1 std)

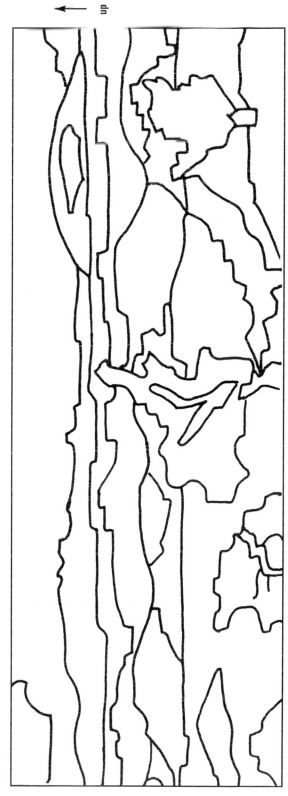

single thread of Kaalund Wool 2468 variegated green. Work the small banksia branches at the bottom left in Wheat stitch with 1 strand of Madeira Silk 1409 light green.

Centre

Stitch the young banksia flowerheads with a double thread of 8742 pale orange in Straight stitch. Each Straight stitch covers 2 rows of Tent stitch. Repeat this step for the old banksia flowerheads, blending 1 thread of 8411 misty light grey and 1 thread of 8313 sandstone.

At the foot of the banksia are clumps of native

grass, created with a single thread and Straight stitch that radiates from the base of the design. First stitch with 8204 dark grey-green, then 8405 pale olive green, then 8411 misty light grey, making sure that each colour can be seen behind the other. Finally, place a few highlight Straight stitches of Madeira Silk 1409 light green against the trunk of the banksia.

Valley

Work clumps of single-wrap French knots using 1 thread of Kaalund Wool 2468 variegated green on the top half of the valley for the treetops. Then, using the same thread, make radiating clusters of Straight stitch to create the tops of the treeferns. Refer to the chart for placement.

Right side

Work the flowerheads on the banksia trees as for Centre, with a double thread and Straight stitch over 2 rows of Tent stitch.

The cliff edge under the banksia has clumps of native grass. Starting at the top row of the cliff edge, work each clump with a single thread of 8204 dark grey-green in Straight stitch that radiates from one spot. Highlight this with a few stitches of 8405 pale olive green.

For the scattered grasses in front, stagger a few so they do not march in a straight line along the bottom edge of the design. Use 8405 pale olive green first, then 8411 misty light grey, to create each clump of grass, and then add highlight stitches with 1 strand each of Madeira Silk 1409 light green. Finally, scatter some highlight stitches, to add depth, with 1 strand of Madeira Silk 1603 mid green.

Red Waratah

Tent stitch, French knots, thread blending

On the edge of a Blue Mountains escarpment, where the wind blows rough and tumble, the red waratah glows against a deep blue sky. In the distance the Three Sisters, a group of stony outcrops steeped in dreamtime myth, sit peacefully, dredged in a pale blue eucalyptus haze.

This needlepoint captures a point of the sun's daily traverse when the colours are fresh, deep and exotic.

Requirements

30 cm x 30 cm square of white 18 count Zweigart
   interlock canvas
Waterproof pen
Ruler
Tapestry needle no. 24

Threads

DMC Medicis Wool, 1 skein of each

Noir black	8413 leaf green
8104 russet	8417 green
8122 dark plum	8419 verdant green
8126 dark red	8420 pale green
8127 red	8427 pale blue
8304 mustard	8500 charcoal
8306 dark brown	8514 dark sand
8346 grass green	8515 oatmeal
8402 olive green	8798 mid sea blue
8403 dark olive green	8845 mid tan
8411 misty light grey	8996 deep azure blue

Madeira Silk, 1 skein of each

0210 red	1603 mid green

Method

Centre the design under the canvas and rule the border. Check the placement of the design to make sure it is straight. Continue to copy the rest of the design.

Chart 1: Background, foreground and border

Follow the colour chart for the position of each background section. Tent stitch in horizontal rows. Use 2 threads of Medicis Wool, and where 2 skeins are recorded blend one thread of each colour in the needle. For the border Tent stitch 3 rows in Noir.

Chart 2: Waratah and bushes

Before starting, read all the special stitching instructions for the leaves, stem, flower and bushes. Complete all areas of Tent stitch before starting the French knots.

Waratah leaves

Tent stitch each leaf's edges, centre veins and lower stalks with 8419 verdant green. Then work the

Chart 1: Background, foreground and border

8996

8996 + 8798

8798

8798 + 8427

8798 + 8402

Border
Noir, 3 rows

8411 + 8304

8122 + 8845

8515

8500 + 8515

8514

8402 + 8403

8402

8402 + 8413

8346

Chart 2: Waratah and bushes

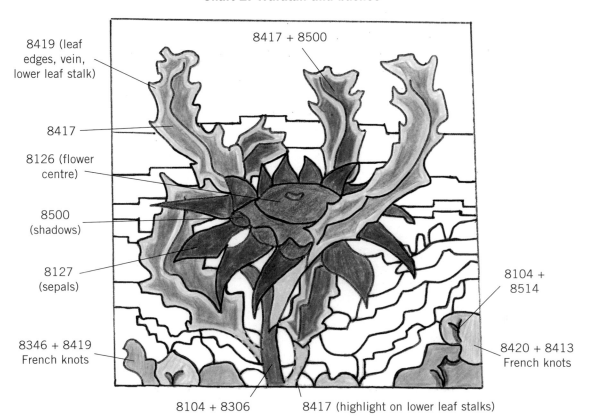

8419 (leaf
edges, vein,
lower leaf stalk)

8417 + 8500

8417

8126 (flower
centre)

8500
(shadows)

8127
(sepals)

8104 +
8514

8346 + 8419
French knots

8420 + 8413
French knots

8104 + 8306

8417 (highlight on lower leaf stalks)

Chart 3 Flower centre: raised stitches

1603 + 0210 single-wrap French knots (1 strand of each)

0210 double-wrap French knots (2 strands)

0210 single-wrap French knots (2 strands)

Outline

three leaves that are stitched in 8417 green. For the other two leaves blend 1 thread of 8417 with 1 of 8500 charcoal.

Use 1 thread of 8417 and small Straight stitches to highlight the edges of the two lower leaf stalks.

Waratah stem
Tent stitch the stem, blending 1 thread of 8104 russet and 1 of 8306 dark brown.

Waratah flower
Tent stitch all areas of the flower centre with a double thread of 8126 dark red. Next, stitch the shadow areas between the flower centre and the base of the sepals with 8500 charcoal. Then work the sepals with 8127 red.

Foreground cliff edge bushes
Tent stitch the branches of the bush in the foreground, blending 1 thread of 8104 russet and 1 of 8514 dark sand. To create a raised effect for the bushes leaning over the edge of the cliff, make as many French knots as you can fit into the space (you may find that this will partly obscure the branches of the bushes).

The bushes are worked in two colour groups, and both are blends. Alternate these blends as you work from left to right along the bushes (use 1 thread of each colour):
8346 grass green + 8419 verdant green
8420 pale green + 8413 leaf green

Chart 3: Flower centre: raised stitches

The smallest circle in the flower centre is covered by tiny, single-wrap French knots made by blending 1 strand of Madeira Silk 1603 mid green and 1 strand of Madeira Silk 0210 red (6 knots in total).

The next circle features single-wrap French knots using 2 strands of Madeira silk 0210. For the rest of the flower centre make double-wrap French knots in 2 strands of Madeira Silk 0210.

Summer Escape

Tent stitch, Straight stitch, Long stitch, French knots, Bullion knot, thread blending.

This is a postcard from paradise. It holds the shimmer of a summer's day when the best way to escape the heat is to swim in the surf. This is the beach where our favourite holidays and wonderful childhood memories are set. The design is easy to draw, and features silk and cotton threads to produce a shimmer effect.

Requirements

22 x 25 cm piece of white 18 count Zweigart interlock canvas
Waterproof pen
No. 24 tapestry needle
No. 10 crewel needle (or as fine as you can manage)

Threads

Madeira Mouline, 1 skein of each
  0213 red
  0408 deep pink
  1103 dark blue
  1307 mid green
  1308 light green
  1503 dark green
  2012 light tan
  2401 white
  2508 grey-blue
Madeira Silk
  0306 pale pink (1 skein)
  1001 frost (1 skein)
  1104 pale blue (2 skeins)
  1105 sea blue (2 skeins)
  2014 cream (1 skein)

Madeira Decora, 1 skein of each
  1466 yellow
  1475 blue

Method

Centre the outline under the canvas and rule up the sides with a waterproof pen. Check your placement of the design, then trace the rest of it. Next, mark where the sky changes colour. Do not rule lines across the design, but mark the outer edge as shown on the outline.

To create subtle blends and graduations of colour a technique known as *thread stripping* is

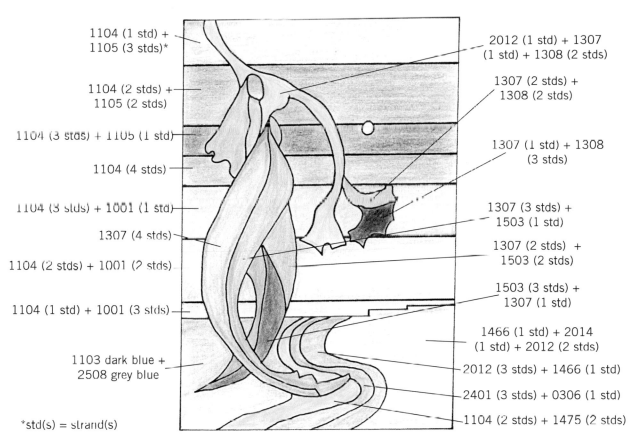

1104 (1 std) +
1105 (3 stds)*

1104 (2 stds) +
1105 (2 stds)

1104 (3 stds) + 1105 (1 std)

1104 (4 stds)

1104 (3 stds) + 1001 (1 std)

1307 (4 stds)

1104 (2 stds) + 1001 (2 stds)

1104 (1 std) + 1001 (3 stds)

1103 dark blue +
2508 grey blue

*std(s) = strand(s)

2012 (1 std) + 1307
(1 std) + 1308 (2 stds)

1307 (2 stds) +
1308 (2 stds)

1307 (1 std) + 1308
(3 stds)

1307 (3 stds) +
1503 (1 std)

1307 (2 stds) +
1503 (2 stds)

1503 (3 stds) +
1307 (1 std)

1466 (1 std) + 2014
(1 std) + 2012 (2 stds)

2012 (3 stds) + 1466 (1 std)

2401 (3 stds) + 0306 (1 std)

1104 (2 stds) + 1475 (2 stds)

employed: the thread is stripped (split) into separate strands. To do this, hold a twist of thread between forefinger and thumb and with the other hand gently pull out a single strand until it is free. Repeat with each remaining strand. The strands can then be ironed, as suggested in the instructions for the leaf, stem and flower cups, as this gives them a straight, flat texture. However, it is not necessary to iron the single strand used for the stamens of the flowers. Nor should you iron the thread blends for the wet and dry sand and for the ocean and surge zones, because these benefit from the chance nature of the twist in the thread.

Start with the sky, and work from top to bottom in horizontal rows in Tent stitch. Use 4 strands of thread for stitching and always check the colour chart for the correct blend of threads.

Sky

Madeira Silk is worked in Tent stitch from top to bottom. Do not iron thread.

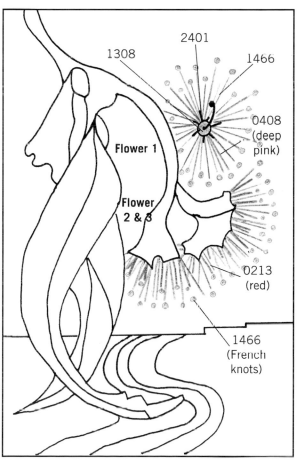

1308

2401

1466

0408
(deep
pink)

Flower 1

Flower
2 & 3

0213
(red)

1466
(French
knots)

Ocean and beach
Tent stitch. Do not iron thread.

Stem and flower cups
Madeira Mouline is used here, in diagonal Long stitch. Iron the threads.

Leaves
Madeira Mouline is used here, in diagonal Long stitch. Iron the threads.

Flowers

Flower 1
First Tent stitch the flower centre with 4 strands of Mouline 1308 light green. Then, using 1 strand of Mouline 0213 red and Straight stitches that radiate from the flower centre, make evenly spaced stitches that are close, but not quite touching. Next, stitch a second layer of slightly shorter Straight stitches over the first layer with 1 strand of Mouline 0408 deep pink. Add a third layer with 1 strand of Mouline 2401 white and much shorter stitches to highlight the centre.

Use 1 strand of Decora 1466 yellow to make the single-wrap French knots and scatter them on and around the edge of the flower.

The style (protruding from Flower 1 centre) is created with a 20-wrap Bullion knot in 1 strand of Mouline 2401 white on a fine crewel needle (no. 10).

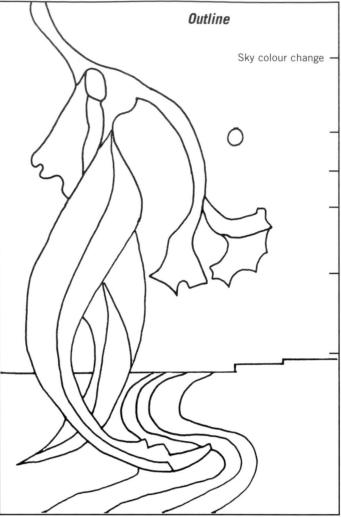

Outline

Sky colour change

layer of shorter Straight stitches on top with 1 strand of Mouline 0213 red. This reverses the colour order of Flower 1 because we are looking at the flower from the side.

Scatter French knots in 1 strand of Decora 1466 yellow along the fringe of the stitches.

Flowers 2 and 3
Create a skirt of colour using Straight stitch and 1 strand of Mouline 0408 deep pink, then place a

Rainforest

Tent stitch, Long stitch, Straight stitch, French knots, Bullion knots, painting

A mongst the sheltered steep-sided ridges that crowd the gently sloping plain of the Sydney basin, pockets of rainforest remain. I grew up in one of these. My playground was a creek hidden by ferns and overhung by tall blue gums, tree ferns, vines and creepers of various sorts.

This version is simpler than the original, which won Highly Commended for my first Sydney Royal Easter Show entry. Read all the instructions before commencing.

Requirements
20 cm x 30 cm white Zweigart interlock canvas
Waterproof pen
Ruler
Jo Sonja's acrylic paint, Hookers green
Jo Sonja's Textile Medium
No. 24 tapestry needle

Threads
DMC Medicis Wool, 1 skein of each

8104 russet	8341 light lime green
8124 tan	8344 tropical green
8300 earth	8419 verdant green
8309 bottle green	8420 pale green
8320 chestnut	8506 dark slate
8322 camel	8838 dark mushroom
8323 dark tan	8846 warm putty

Madeira Mouline, 1 skein of each

1014 pale blue	1308 light green	1503 dark green	2310 dark blush
1101 ice blue	1311 moss	1504 olive	2400 black
1213 clover	1312 bush green	**Madeira Silk,** 1 skein of each	
1305 ivy	1407 grass green	1105 sea blue	1803 grey
1307 mid green	1408 oak	1708 gravel	

Outline

Madeira Decora, 1 skein of each

  1448 grass green   1570 green shadow

Method

Centre the design outline underneath the canvas and rule up the border, following the weft and warp threads of the canvas. As this is a complex design, work from the top down at a leisurely pace and allow the pen to move freely over the canvas. Towards the end, with the pen-free hand holding the canvas in position, lift the edge of the canvas a centimetre or two so that any missed lines can be seen and drawn.

Painting

As this work has large areas of Long stitch, it is wise to paint a pale green wash over those areas in case the thread does not give adequate cover. Mix a pea-sized amount of Hooker's green with 5 mL of water and a drop of textile medium to make a pale green wash (refer to Chapter 3 for more about painting).

Stitching

The directions are set out as a stitch scheme rather than one that follows individual elements of the design. This is essential as the Rainforest project has delicate Long stitching and two layers of stitching in some areas. Complete all of Chart 1 before stitching Charts 2 and 3.

Chart 1: Tent stitch and Wheat Stitch

Start from the top of the design and work down in horizontal rows. Work on one area (e.g. sky, earth etc) at a time, and keep the threads for each blend separate. Please note that many of the thread blends combine three shades.

Sky and Earth

Tent stitch

Follow Chart 1 for colour placement.

Staghorn fronds

These hang down from the tree trunk in the top right-hand corner, each worked in Wheat stitch with 4 strands of Mouline. Two fronds are stitched with 1407 grass green; the far right frond with 1408 oak; and the lowest frond in 1312 bush green.

Treefern

Tent stitch along the outline of the treefern fronds with a double thread of Medicis Wool 8419 verdant green. Tent stitch the top section of the treefern trunk (just below the three fiddleheads of uncurled fronds), with a double thread of Medicis Wool 8309 bottle green.

Chart 1: Tent stitch and Wheat stitch

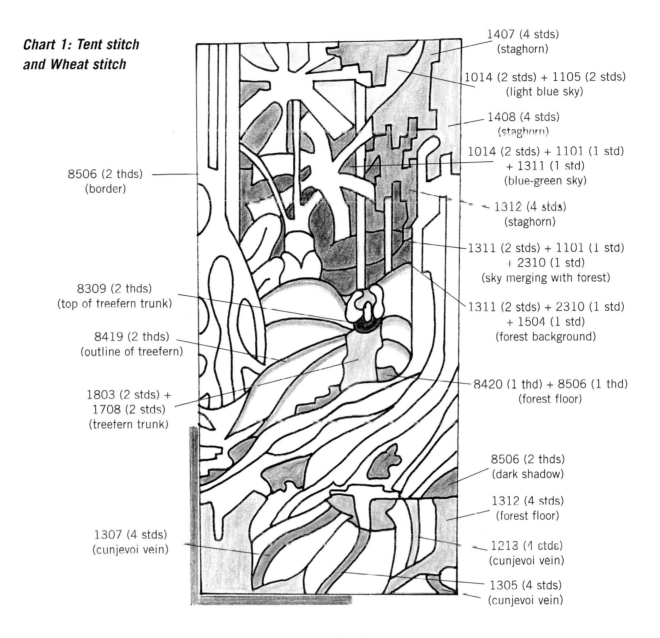

1407 (4 stds)
(staghorn)

1014 (2 stds) + 1105 (2 stds)
(light blue sky)

1408 (4 stds)
(staghorn)

1014 (2 stds) + 1101 (1 std)
+ 1311 (1 std)
(blue-green sky)

1312 (4 stds)
(staghorn)

1311 (2 stds) + 1101 (1 std)
+ 2310 (1 std)
(sky merging with forest)

1311 (2 stds) + 2310 (1 std)
+ 1504 (1 std)
(forest background)

8420 (1 thd) + 8506 (1 thd)
(forest floor)

8506 (2 thds)
(dark shadow)

1312 (4 stds)
(forest floor)

1213 (4 stds)
(cunjevoi vein)

1305 (4 stds)
(cunjevoi vein)

8506 (2 thds)
(border)

8309 (2 thds)
(top of treefern trunk)

8419 (2 thds)
(outline of treefern)

1803 (2 stds) +
1708 (2 stds)
(treefern trunk)

1307 (4 stds)
(cunjevoi vein)

Work the main body of the treefern trunk in Tent stitch, with a Madeira Silk blend: 2 strands of 1803 grey and 2 strands of 1708 gravel.

Cunjevoi

These tall fleshy plants, also called Elephant's Ears, grow on the rainforest floor. The wide centre vein of four of the leaves is in Tent stitch; for the fifth leaf (underside view), see Chart 2. Use 4 strands of Mouline and, working from left to right, Tent stitch the first leaf with 1307 mid green, the second with 1305 ivy, the third with 1213 clover and the last with 1305.

Border

Using 2 threads of Medicis Wool 8506 dark slate, Tent stitch a border 2 rows deep on all sides.

Chart 2: Long stitch

Left tree trunk

Vine. Blend 1 thread of Medicis Wool 8322 camel and 1 of 8420 pale green. To make the vine appear rounded, use padded Long stitch by working a vertical Long stitch in each section and then overstitch with short horizontal stitches. This also gives the vine height and lifts it away from the trunk.

8341 (2 thds)
(upper palm frond)

8322 (1 thd) + 8420 (1 thd)
(vine)

8124 (2 thds)
(tree trunk)

8838 (2 thds)
(palm branches)

1308 (6 stds)
(birdsnest fern)

8838 (1 thd) + 8323 (1 thd)
(palm trunk)

1503 (6 stds)
(birdsnest fern)

8320 (1 thd) followed by
8341 (2 thds) (treefern)

1312 (4 stds)
(sapling)

1307 (4 stds)
(cunjevoi)

8846 (2 thds)
(tree trunks)

8419 (1 thd)
+ 8344 (1 thd)
(lower palm frond)

8322 (2 thds)
(tree trunk)

8124 (2 thds)
(tree trunk)

8323 (2 thds)
(tree trunk)

8300 (2 thds)
(tree roots)

1503 (4 stds
(cunjevoi)

1312 (4 stds)
(cunjevoi)

1305 (4 stds)
(cunjevoi)

Chart 2: Long stitch

Tree trunk. Work 2 threads of Medicis Wool 8124 tan in a horizontal stitch.

Birdsnest fern. Long stitch the upper frond with 6 strands of Mouline 1308 light green. The extra 2 strands give a slightly padded effect.

Birdsnest fern. Long stitch lower frond with 6 strands of Mouline 1503 dark green.

Palm tree

Palm trunk. Blend 1 thread of Medicis Wool 8838 dark mushroom and 1 of 8323 dark tan. Stitch the branches in 2 threads of Medicis Wool 8838. Note

that the trunk consists of two sections: stitch each one separately.

Upper palm frond. Use 2 threads of Medicis Wool 8341 light lime green.

Lower palm frond. Blend 1 thread of Medicis Wool 8419 verdant green and 1 of 8344 tropical green.

Distant tree trunks

Use padded Long stitch. Add dimension here, too, by using a vertical Long stitch, overstitched with short horizontal stitches in 2 threads of Medicis Wool 8846 warm putty.

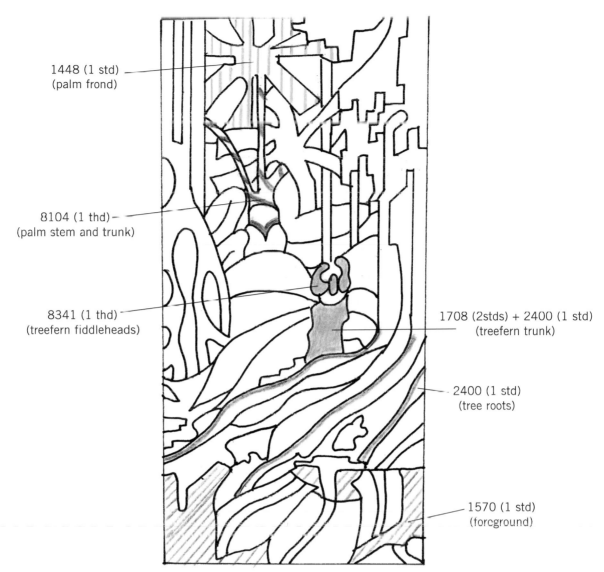

1448 (1 std)
(palm frond)

8104 (1 thd)
(palm stem and trunk)

8341 (1 thd)
(treefern fiddleheads)

1708 (2stds) + 2400 (1 std)
(treefern trunk)

2400 (1 std)
(tree roots)

1570 (1 std)
(foreground)

Chart 3: Topstitching

Sapling

The young tree at the foot of the left tree trunk is stitched with 4 strands of Mouline 1312 bush green. Stitch a vertical row of Tent stitch up the centre of the tree, then use diagonal Long stitch to create its leaves on either side.

Treefern

Two layers of Long stitch are made to fill in the fronds. This gives them bulk, and shows a glimpse of the older, desiccated fronds beneath. First stitch with a single thread of Medicis Wool 8320 chestnut in long even stitches, then go over the same area with a double thread of Medicis Wool 8341 light lime green. Stitch loosely, allowing the thread to sit on top without pulling it at the end of each stitch. Use the needle to push the top thread aside, to give a peek at what lies underneath.

Right tree trunk and tree roots

These are all stitched with 2 threads of Medicis Wool in Long stitch, with a diagonal slope similar to Tent stitch.

Foreground – cunjevoi

Work diagonal Long stitches sloping to the left, with 4 strands of Mouline 1307 mid green.

Work diagonal Long stitches sloping to the left, with 4 strands of Mouline 1305 ivy. Note that the leaf at the bottom right-hand corner is stitched in the opposite direction.

Use horizontal Long stitch with 4 strands of Mouline 1503 dark green for this underside view of the leaf.

Work diagonal Long stitches in both directions with Mouline 1312 bush green.

Chart 3: Topstitching

This chart is completed last of all to add delicate highlights.

Palm frond

Work 1 strand of Decora 1448 grass green in Straight stitch, stitched vertically, missing every alternate stitch.

Palm stem and trunk

Work 1 thread of Medicis Wool 8104 russet, wrapped around the stem at evenly spaced intervals. Outline the 'V' in the middle of the trunk with small Straight stitches.

Treefern fiddleheads

Create these on top of the treefern trunk with 3 Bullion knots, using 1 thread of Medicis Wool 8341 light lime green. Working from left to right, the first knot has 15 wraps, the second has only 10 wraps, and the third is large, with 20 wraps. This third knot is extra long so that it can end in a curl or a rounded question-mark shape.

Treefern trunk

The single-wrap French knots are made with 2 strands of Madeira Silk 1708 gravel and 1 strand of Mouline 2400 black, randomly placed on the treefern trunk.

Tree root outline

Work a series of single long Straight stitches in 1 strand of Mouline 2400 black to follow the spreading roots of this forest tree (right side of the design); they will not be too obvious, but still add bulk to the tree.

Foreground

Use a single strand of Decora 1570 green shadow in a diagonal Long stitch.